THE
MODERN
COMPASSIONATE
LEADER

12 Essential Characteristics of the Rising Sales Leader

THE
MODERN
COMPASSIONATE
LEADER

**12 Essential Characteristics
of the Rising Sales Leader**

JAMES MICHAEL MARTIN

Publisher Info:
JMM Leadership Press
14720 Sorrel Run
Broomfield, CO 80023.

Because of the dynamic nature of the Internet, any web addresses or links contained in this book may have changed since publication and may no longer be valid. The views expressed in this work are solely those of the author.

Dedication Photo Credit: Gordon Garvey
Book Design: YellowStudios
Editor: Alexandra O'Connell

www.moderncompassionateleader.com

Printed in the United States of America
First printing: September 2017

Paperback ISBN: 978-0-9987254-2-0
Hardcover ISBN: 978-0-9987254-0-6
Library of Congress Control Number: 2017903132

This book is dedicated to
my friend and colleague Joseph "Rick" Bancroft.

A true compassionate leader who engendered respect
and love from everyone he encountered, Rick made
the world a better place one relationship at a time.

CONTENTS

Part III — Conclusion

Preface

> *"I am committed to my personal journey of enhancing the lives of others, through being my best, and sharing myself."*
> — *Jim Martin*

Thank the Lord! Another book on management and leadership. There aren't enough of those.

Not really. This isn't another one of those books. And while there are twelve characteristics, it's not a twelve-step guide to leadership either.

This book is for you. You, the rising leader in a sales organization who has just been promoted from top performer to team leader. You, the leader with a few years of management under your belt who has hit a flat spot in producing results with your team. You, the leader navigating organizational change and searching for the right combination of skills to unlock the potential of your newly formed team. You, the aspiring leader producing good results, ready to make the next step into leadership.

This book is for all of you. All of you who want to make a difference in the lives of those around you by lifting them higher with a leadership style of competence and compassion. You, the Modern Compassionate Leader.

This book will not teach you how to be Jack Welch or Steve Jobs. There are plenty of those books already. You see, I was also once an aspiring manager, a rising leader. I read those books. *Here are the 5 or 10 or 50 things great CEOs do. If you do these things too, you'll rise to CEO yourself. Just follow the formula.*

If you're looking for a book about ladder climbing to the top of your organization, this is probably not your book. There's nothing wrong with that aspiration. But the reality is that most of us fortunate enough to lead sales teams will not become CEO. We'll have no books written about us or TV interviews about our secret sauce to make it to the top.

The fact is that the tools required to be a successful CEO are not the same tools you as a sales leader need to win in the marketplace every day. They are not the same tools you need to build a healthy and productive team. Nor are they the tools you need to handle all the responsibilities and pressures you face to meet your goals, satisfy your customers, and help your people develop in their careers. I assert that you, the sales leader, have the most difficult job in any sales organization.

You stand at the crossroads of authority and accountability. The intersection of how things get done in your company. Performing your job with grace and integrity and with the well-being of others in mind is what this book is all about.

I've spent thirty years in sales and sixteen of those years in management. I've learned the lessons offered in this book in the same ways you learn. I've worked for managers who were effective and who had positive influence on me. I've worked for others who were less effective. And I've worked for managers who were a little of both.

As a person who was given an unexpected opportunity to lead others, I am no different than you. I did some things well, some things not so well, and some things OK. A lifelong learner, I tried to pay attention to the lessons presented to me all the while. I continuously refined my approach based on my experiences, feedback from my team members and colleagues, and guidance from mentors and others who cared about me.

With this humility, I offer you my recommendation on how you can become The Modern Compassionate Leader you want to be. My personal mission statement above is the compass I'll use to guide you there.

Thank you for reading.

James Martin
May 2017

Introduction

Welcome to *The Modern Compassionate Leader*. Before you dive in, let me first provide you with a few disclaimers. **This is not a think tank research book about management theory.**

While I have some external references in these chapters, this book is different from many business books you may have read. There is no research staff surveying companies to identify broadly applied best practices and conventional wisdom. I didn't interview CEOs at Fortune 500 companies to come up with the principles herein. There is no empirical research propping up my assertions about what it means to be an effective and compassionate leader.

This book contains my opinions. My beliefs about leading others in a way that appreciates everyone in an organization as a complete person. As more than just a name on a roster, or as an employee's most recent performance review, or as a workplace-only organism that serves the leader in a purely utilitarian manner. This book presents my core understanding of how to become an effective and empathetic leader of human persons. You are welcome to disagree with my thinking.

I believe in my heart that the guidance I give you in this book works, based on my own experience.

There are other competencies that are important for managers.

No question about that. To lead in a business organization today is a complex endeavor. Many skills are required to succeed. Business has become so intense, so specialized, and so competitive. You must develop strengths that are unique to the business in which you compete. You must seek out other resources to build the repertoire of abilities you need to win in your specific marketplace.

The twelve competencies I talk about represent the essential hard and soft skills that I believe all managers of sales professionals and sales processes need to lead effectively. These are the essential tools. Your tool box is only so big. I selected a dozen areas of competence because I think these will fit inside the tool box you carry every day in your role as sales leader. These skills also represent the group of competencies where you do not want gaps. In my view, serious gaps in any of these twelve skills can lead to career derailment.

Is everything I need to know to be successful as a modern compassionate leader in this book?

Of course not. There is no way to provide you with every-thing you need to know in this limited space. Furthermore, no static vehicle such as a book can suffice as an end-to-end reference for everything you need to know to succeed in your hyper-dynamic environment. It's not a realistic expectation to think you've got all you need to know in the palm of your hand.

This book is your starting point. I intend to raise your awareness of the need to become competent across each of the twelve areas of focus. I want to stimulate you to conduct a personal assessment of your knowledge, experience, and habits during each chapter. Recognize gaps. Note discomfort around your current approaches. Recognize your tendencies for self-deception. Get really honest with yourself. Use this as your opportunity to pursue learning and enlightenment to elevate your game as leader.

Now that the disclaimers are out of the way, let me talk about how the book is designed to help you.

The twelve chapters are loosely divided between hard and soft competencies. The first six chapters are mostly about hard skills. The final six are mostly about soft skills. Mostly. No skills are completely intellectual and no skills are completely emotional. There is overlap.

The terms hard and soft are troublesome to me. Especially in the business world, hard skills have been traditionally valued more than soft skills. That is slowly evolving, but it is still true that new hires are screened for hard skills in overwhelming proportion over soft skills. You need both and I'll make that case to you in the pages that follow.

The chapters in the book are structured in a specific format.

First, I'll share a story from my experience that illustrates the need for the skill. My stories will sometimes demonstrate when I used the skill myself or observed the skill being used effectively. They will sometimes illustrate when I missed the mark.

Second, I'll point out recognizable situations, behaviors, and lessons so you can see when you'll need to apply the skill effectively. These examples are provided so you can relate the concept to something you may have already experienced in your career, or perhaps a challenge you haven't seen yet.

Finally, I'll guide you on how to access additional learning to strengthen the skill. I'll try to get you pointed in the right direction so you can pursue your own development in each area of focus.

The book is structured in this way so you can read it from cover to cover if you'd like, or you can pick it up and focus on just one chapter if that's what you have time for today. It is also a resource you can return to as you encounter situations calling for a specific skill. Use it as your refresher so you can react to situations with your most attentive and responsive self.

I intend to open your eyes and your mind with my thinking. Many people in my life helped me in each of these competencies. I often wished that all of that support could be consolidated into a single resource for me. This book is my wish for the same for you.

Lead well.

PART I

The Hard Skills

ONE

Strategic Thinking

*"Perception is strong and sight weak. In strategy it is
important to see distant things as if they were close and
to take a distanced view of close things."*
— Miyamoto Musashi

Welcome to the start of your journey to becoming a compassionate leader. We start with strategic thinking, because this is the launchpad for everything else you do as a leader. This is your opportunity to place all of your skill development into the context of your greater career purpose, your mission. Becoming skilled at defining, communicating, and coalescing others around a common strategy is the cornerstone of your leadership brand. It separates leaders from managers. Strategic thinkers attract followers, supporters, and allies. So get up on your toes and look out over the horizon. Your journey is underway.

A Team's First Steps

As a pre-teen boy, my backyard was a distinctive place where my formative thinking developed in a progression of small choices. A three hundred square foot concrete patio abutted our house, protruding into the yard. A row of varied flower beds bordered the left side and stretched eighty feet to the rear property line, the last twenty feet bordered by our neighbor's white stucco garage. A solid row of forsythia extended forty feet along the back property line to the right. Bright yellow in spring, it transformed into a tangled green jungle by summer. Stretching back to the house on the right border was a line of twenty-foot high arborvitaes reaching back to the patio, anchored finally by a giant birch tree next to the house. Inside these borders stood a massive lilac bush, ten feet in diameter, as well as a substantial vegetable garden. Despite these obstacles, my friends and I managed to carve out football and WiffleBall fields. It was a special place to me.

Birds and insects loved our backyard. The flowers and endless nesting spots made it a great place for them to hang out. When I was a boy there were at least a few times when my friends and I encountered a bee or wasp nest. Bees loved the space between the concrete patio and the dirt below, and wasps loved the many trees and bushes on which to anchor their paper nests. My friends and I stayed busy in that yard. And our imaginations were at the ready.

If we sprayed the bees' nest with the hose, would we be able to run faster than the bees will chase us? What if we hit the wasp nest with the bat? How many wasps are in there anyway?

I was not a fast runner. I had never outrun any of my friends. As much as I wanted to see what would happen, I understood my role, and my survival strategy was obvious to me. I could not be the trigger man. I needed to begin two steps further from the target than my friends to have a chance to stay unscathed. Strategic thinking at age twelve. There always seemed to be one friend who thought about this question less strategically. I was never stung.

I've always had a capacity for strategic thinking. That basic consideration of the consequences of the actions you take before you act, based on your understanding of the critical factors. The ability to step into the future scene, and experience that scene in a fully sensing manner.

Presumably, the older we get, the further our horizons stretch when considering consequences for our options, choices, and actions. We think about where to attend college, whether or not to exercise, to marry and have children, to purchase a home, to pursue a productive career, and how and when to retire. Sometimes there are strong emotional and environmental factors that influence these choices. Our visualization of these and other life options paint our picture of the future. We imagine ourselves in that picture, and decide which strategy choices to pursue to create our reality.

In the fall of 2012 the sales division was kicking off a new fiscal year and a new selling year. During what was also the culmination of a comprehensive organizational restructure initiative, my fellow leaders and I were launching brand new teams. I met my new national food service team for the first time late on a Monday afternoon. At the end of a day of company-wide meetings outlining the structures of the new teams, the rationale for the changes that were taking place, and the new assignments for each of the employees, I got the chance to address my team for the very first time.

I wasn't the only one. Roughly a dozen leaders were simultaneously meeting with their teams for the first time. Some of our people had anchored our prior teams, and others were transitioning in. All had a brand new job description and a new set of responsibilities. By late afternoon people were in a zombie-like daze, consumed with thoughts about how these changes would impact them personally, and little else.

As leaders, we were on our own to determine the best way to start our relationship with our new teams. I could see that my fellow managers were adopting consistent approaches. Review their annual operating plan, quarterly objectives, and individual performance measures. Hand out KPIs and call their teams to action. No time to waste. Get their teams right into the work. They reviewed sales metrics, top customers, and other key business drivers. These teams had one clear distinction from my own. They were organized against established channels of business, while my team would pioneer growth in a long-ignored channel.

We could not have found ourselves in a less inspiring setting. A windowless, overheated conference room. The room had been configured to be thirty feet wide by sixty feet long. And while the measurements resembled my backyard from long ago, the borders were far less appealing. Textured moveable walls that held dust and squelched creativity. Round cloth-covered tables surrounded by eight cramped and uncomfortable chairs stretched from front to back. A utility cart with a laptop and projector pointed at a large white screen in front completed the scene. No attractive places to nest. Nothing to stare at to spark imagination. No daydreaming permitted here, just business. Ladies and gentlemen, inspiration has left the building.

Instinctively, I knew I had to elevate the mindset of my team. I needed them up at 50,000 feet, where I stood, to see the landscape and imagine where we would take the business over the next ten years. There was no guarantee any of us would be with the company ten years later, but I felt our strategic vision needed to look out that far to guide the decisions we would make together. We had to break out of the moment and the heaviness of the organizational changes everyone was now digesting, and get this team on a mission. Given our physical environment, I needed to stimulate the collective imagination. We needed to get into purely aligned strategic thinking. It was a tall challenge.

I looked at my team. They were visibly anxious. Though I had ninety minutes, my meeting was brief: thirty minutes. I ditched the PowerPoint presentation I had carefully prepared with the same content as my peers. I addressed my team of thirty-five people informally. I went around the room and allowed everyone a chance to speak. Those who had worked together on my teams shared how positive and rewarding our prior successes had been. How we had worked together as a team and helped each other to grow. How much fun winning had been. The faces of the veterans in the room slowly began to light up. New team members, weary from the grueling day, began to sit taller and listen intently. There was a calm excitement building and it began to spread. It felt like something might be different here.

One by one, I asked each person how many years of experience they had in the food business. We tallied more than three hundred years of collective experience, with specialization from nearly every segment of our business, and additional experience in many other related businesses. We didn't just have a team, we had an all-star team. If any team could win in the marketplace, this one could. Now my own excitement was building. I had chosen this team. I knew their competence. But now I started to feel their passion. I thought we could do something special.

I asked them to picture us together in the scene of our future success. I told them that together, we would craft the strategy for food service sales success for the company, and then we would pursue that strategy with full commitment to winning in the marketplace. We would be the business and the sales team that people would talk about. We would be the place where people wanted to work. We would capture the excitement of the company. We intended to lead and win and we were going to do it all together as a unit. I talked about the difference we would make as a team, not the money we would make as individuals.

I told them how committed I was to each of them. As individuals and as a team. I told them they were each on the team because I wanted them here. Then I made it personal. I shared my own mission statement:

I am committed to my personal journey of enhancing the lives of others, through being my best, and sharing myself.

Finally, I challenged them to do two things. I said if each of us worked on learning and being better each day than we were the day before, and we supported each other to do that, there was no way we would lose. I promised to do that and asked for the same in return. We committed to each other and adjourned.

Soon after that first meeting, my management team and I decided to hold a strategy summit. We included members from the team, functional colleagues across the enterprise, and other key supporters and influencers. The price of admission to the summit was to read and understand the situation analysis the management team had drafted, and to come prepared to think and work hard together.

The summit was energizing and productive. We authored an extensive analysis of our business and our opportunities, and carved our strategy from that assessment. When we were done, we had constructed a coherent plan against our strategy, and we began executing. All the summit participants contributed to the strategy, and our team's support system was now expanding rapidly. We were acquiring fans. People wanted us to succeed and they wanted to be associated with our successes. They wanted in.

Within three months, we had a strategy to grow our business and win in the marketplace. We hired the remaining team members we needed, trained them on the strategy and infused them with our collective passion. Ultimately we added millions of dollars in new business to the company in our first two years. We partnered with exciting new customers, and became a focal point for growth opportunities in the company's wholesale business.

Long after that first meeting, as I was departing from the company, I was stunned and delighted to hear from people who repeated back to me my exact words from that first day. My mission statement. My call to action. My focus on learning and supporting each other. They were simple words and they had made an impact because they were real. I believed them and invited others to believe with me. They made a difference.

If I hadn't invited my team into that picture on our first day together, to look beyond those windowless walls, to envision the future and place themselves into that scene I imagined, our successes would have been muted. We would have depended too heavily on top performers, and spent too many managerial hours getting everyone on the same page and heading in the same direction. But we started with common strategic thinking. Our success became real because we created our intended outcomes together.

STRATEGIC THINKING: RECOGNIZE IT

What is Strategic Thinking?

So what does it mean to be strategic? To be a strategic thinker?

Eavesdrop on any conference room where a hiring team is considering a candidate for selection into a leadership role. You'll hear the questions. *Is she strategic, or is she tactical? Can he rise above the team and take a strategic approach to the big problems? Does she have the ability to look at difficult situations holistically like we do? Can he operate at 50,000 feet?*

Often, notions of strategy invoke images of warfare. That's not what we're talking about here. Business is not war, and it's always bothered me when people draw that analogy. In basic terms, strategy is what you want to accomplish, and tactics are how you're going to go about doing it.

Whether you are authoring or implementing plans, consider the following two strategic thinking opportunities and your role in each.

Authoring and activating strategy

To think strategically requires a strategy. I know, that sounds obvious. Strategic thinking requires an awareness and an intent to become the future state you envision. The weight of this burden falls disproportionately on the leader's shoulders. In the busy-ness of day-to-day activities and responsibilities of the team members, the leader must be able to raise her head above the commotion, see the intended destination derived from the strategy, and continuously assess whether or not the team is on course. She must either drive the team forward or correct course to guide her team in the direction of the finish line.

As a leader in the middle of your organization, it is unlikely you'll have just one strategy. Your company has a singular mission statement, but your contribution to fulfilling that mission consists of a portfolio of strategies. Depending on your business, those may be closely related or loosely linked. But achieving all of them is your charge.

Your strategies may emerge from any number of methodologies. They may be handed to you from senior leadership. You may develop them through collaborative thinking with stakeholders in your company. Or, you may be tasked with putting your head down by yourself or with your team to come up with them. Regardless of their genesis, articulating them effectively and gaining alignment with your team and others in your company is fundamental to your success. At any moment, each person who supports the achievement of the strategies must be able to recite them, explain what they mean, and understand the critical actions required to achieve them.

In my experience, writing the perfect strategic statement tends to take on too much time and deliberation. Don't get me wrong. These need to be clear and powerful statements of intention for the business owners. There should be no ambiguity in interpretation about what they mandate. At the same time, these are living words. They reflect the intention of the company and team at a moment in time, based on the best information that is currently available. The day they are inked, things change. These declarations may be obsolete soon after they are authored. Don't be alarmed by that. Your job is to keep them alive and call for fresh thinking along the way to make sure they reflect the current direction of the business. Write them in pencil and keep a good eraser handy.

Implementing and managing strategy

You, the leader, must keep these strategies top of mind at all times. Every action, question, and challenge you encounter with your team must be held against the strategies you have adopted. Ask relevant questions and prompt your team to do the same.

> ➢ Will this decision move us in the direction of our stated strategy or away from it?
> ➢ By taking this action, are we more or less likely to reach our strategic objective?
> ➢ This opportunity is certainly attractive, but is it on-strategy or off-strategy for us now?

Training your team to think like you in this way is critical to your efficiency and effectiveness as a manager. It doesn't take long to understand if you have strategic thinkers or tacticians on your team. A team full of strategic thinkers can make your job easier. You won't have to intervene on solutions frequently because your team member understands which options are the most strategically relevant. You stay out of the weeds and develop an experienced team that keeps you informed so you can support them on the really big questions.

Good tactics are essential to effective execution. But if your team is too tactical in orientation, you'll find yourself constantly looking over their shoulders to make sure their moves are consistent with your higher order strategies. You'll be quickly undermined as a strategic leader. You'll be involved in far too many details at the ground level. You yourself may become cloudy about your strategic focus. Opportunities that were clearly outside the scope of your strategic plan will appear to be more attractive. Before you know it you and your team will be working on lots of things, but your strategy will drift from your grasp.

A team that is overly tactical becomes reactive and fails to behave in a proactive style. This is a fundamental threat to you and your company. As a leader, you must identify those on your team who have strategic potential and remove those members who are stuck in a tactical world. Once you have a clear assessment on who your strategic players are and who don't make that cut, you must act. This is true in the hiring process as well. Surface strategic characteristics in your new employee screening process and prioritize those as core criteria for qualifying new team members.

Whether you are authoring and activating your own strategy or implementing and executing someone else's, communicate your priorities to your team in a way that ensures you're not the only one losing sleep about them.

STRATEGIC THINKING: APPLY IT

I've seen junior members of organizations demonstrate strategic thinking and I've seen senior members demonstrate little. Strategic thinkers excel in three areas. They understand their own knowledge strengths and gaps, create daily space to think strategically, and intervene when strategic thinking is absent.

You know more than you think you do, but not as much as you could know

Be confident. You are in your role because you have demonstrated an ability to rise above others through your business acumen. Whether you find yourself in a strategic planning conversation or you're just trying to solve something on your plate today, understand this. People look to you, from above, below, and across your organization because they respect your body of work and your subject matter knowledge. Be assertive about contributing your expertise, your perspective, especially at the outset of a strategic planning cycle. Remember, you'll be living with the strategy you agree to for three to five years. Make sure it is something you believe in and can make others embrace.

At the same time, be open to input. Ask for it. When you're sure of yourself, ask for more input. Ask challenge questions to planning panels and functional teams. Make it clear that your knowledge isn't complete, and that you want to learn and drive learning so the strategies and supporting actions can be most effective. I've seen too many leaders, including me, make the mistake of closing down debate too soon in an effort to appear decisive. That stifles input from others and leads to less than optimal outcomes. The more ideas you bring into the room, the better the chances that the best ones will emerge.

Make strategic thinking part of your daily interactions with your team members

Developing strategy is an endeavor that occurs between people. I believe that the bulk of the day for the sales leader should be spent on first-person contact. For me, that means completing my emails and other follow up tasks at the beginning of the day and working on projects at the end of the day. This approach leaves me with around six to eight hours for meetings, one on one conversations, and sales calls. I scan emails during the day to handle anything urgent, but I consider the time I spend talking with my team or other stakeholders to be sacred. I try to avoid the disruptions of the streaming life at all costs so I can maximize focus.

For my team members and close stakeholders, I have a block of time on the calendar for us to talk each week. I let them set the agenda and send it to me before the call. We don't talk about anything but their topics once the call starts, then I introduce anything else we need to discuss after that. We always have extra time to talk about bigger picture topics.

By approaching my day this way, I am able to be a more strategic person. My conversations with my team members or colleagues can go longer, because I'm not pressed by random demands for my time and attention. Because those conversations are extended, we can elevate any topic to 50,000 feet, and talk about it strategically. I instill expansive thinking practice in my team member, and they help me work out my thinking about a strategic level topic. I probe for the pulse on a hot issue, understand my team's mindset on something, or surface a new challenge we should be thinking about.

Build in a conversation plan like this for the most important people in your work world, and you and your team will become much more strategic and in sync with your approach to your business.

Be an interventionist when it comes to strategic thinking

As I said, an abundance of exclusively tactical thinkers around you can undermine your ability to effectively lead and rise in your organization. I've seen it. A manager that gets caught in the weeds is a manager that is limited in his potential for growth and promotion. Recognize if your team is pulling you into too many situations that you need them to solve. Guard against that and counter it by challenging more strategic thinking.

When you signed up to be a leader, you didn't simply agree to think and act strategically in your own duties. You committed to your company to spread leadership qualities and behaviors across your organization. You became a strategic champion for your colleagues and steward of your piece of the company culture. Stepping in when you see a gap in strategic thinking on your team and elsewhere is your duty. Own that.

The strategic leader needs help. He is not a genius. The best leaders can set a strategic course and stay focused on guiding the team on the correct heading. But unless the entire team understands the strategic direction and commits to that same heading, the leader will become exhausted trying to keep everyone aligned, and the team will meander without the compelling intention of reaching its destination. Build your team to achieve your strategy. Make this the foundation of your personal leadership brand. Be known as the strategic leader that consistently delivers your piece of the company's mission.

You are off to a great start. You're up on your toes and you can see further than when we started. Now it's time to get serious about the tangible functional skills you'll need to acquire to lead effectively in all the disciplines you'll touch. It's time to move from intention to execution. It's time to fill your toolbox.

Are you ready to dig in?

TWO

Functional Competence

*"The great obstacle to discovering the shape of the earth,
the continents, and the ocean was not ignorance but the
illusion of knowledge."*

— *Daniel J. Boorstin*

In this chapter, we'll discuss the core functional skills you need. These talents span the disciplines of selling, technical knowledge, people skills, and executive acumen. Mastery in these areas will propel you to leadership success, while gaps can derail your career.

Knowing Just Enough to be Dangerous

Over the course of my career, I sold or led the sales of a wide variety of products. Everything from heavy trucks and component parts, to high precision optical instrumentation and software, to coffee and equipment for food service. Each time I started a new role, I knew little about the products I would be selling, certainly less than the people on the teams I was joining. When I transitioned into management, I had reached a point where my product knowledge was strong, but my grasp of best practices in management was highly theoretical. In each role, I benefited from another person deciding that I held the promise of learning and applying the essential functional skills necessary to be productive in that new role. While I received and appreciated that person's trust, a story from my beginning in sales illustrates how I failed to appreciate my responsibility to build my functional skills.

My first job in sales was working for Mack Trucks, Inc. I didn't know a thing about trucks. Nothing. But the guys I knew that worked there sold a lot of trucks and made a lot of money. They were basically guys like me, so I figured I could do that too. Having grown up near Mack's headquarters in Allentown, Pennsylvania, I was very familiar with the Mack brand. I already knew Mack built the toughest, best trucks around, but I didn't really know why or how they did that. I certainly wasn't ready to explain that to a customer.

The Mack sales training program was second to none. It was a nine-month intensive training program. Nine months! I was selected for the program along with five other trainees. The six of us spent those months learning everything we could about the business, while living and traveling together. We visited and spent time shadowing workers in all the manufacturing plants. We worked in the corporate offices and branches. We trained in the testing centers. We rode with truck drivers. We worked in the service shops and parts departments. We took classroom courses, did homework, and were tested on our knowledge about technical, economic, and functional factors of the truck business and Mack Trucks.

When I graduated from the program I was assigned to a company-operated branch in Philadelphia as a sales representative. I knew everything you could know about the truck business. It was time to sell and make money. I thought.

I got off to a pretty good start. I sold an average of four trucks per month, which generated good commissions. I had cash and I was happy. I didn't realize that my manager was helping me behind the scenes, so each sale made my confidence soar. I just thought I was good. After all, I had learned everything I needed to know in that training program, right?

Soon however, my sales began to dry up. I struggled for several months after my initial surge. While I had occasional good months over the course of my two years as a Mack sales rep, I never really seemed to be doing any better than average. I made a lot of missteps and missed many opportunities. Why was that?

In a nutshell, it was because I stopped learning. My base of knowledge gained from the nine months in training had evaporated in a few months. I stopped paying attention to the things I didn't know. I convinced myself that I knew enough and that success would just happen for me. But it didn't. It didn't happen because I failed to recognize that building my functional skills is a process, not an event.

Building your functional skills isn't something you ever complete. It is more than simply becoming the learning leader that we'll discuss in Chapter Ten. You must master the functional skills to lead from a solid foundation. You're never done. I thought I was. I was cocky about what I thought I knew, and I paid for my overconfidence.

FUNCTIONAL SKILLS: RECOGNIZE IT

Which Functional Skills Do I Need?

This is the essential question for the individual contributor who is transitioning into a leadership role for the first time. But it's also a great gut check question for the leader who wants to take an objective, outside view of herself to understand where she has knowledge gaps. Self-awareness is the key no matter what stage of leadership you find yourself.

It's not my intention to go into deep explanations of each of these skills. I do however want to heighten your awareness to the need to quickly establish a solid foundation of knowledge upon which you can build expertise to support your team and rise as a thought leader in your organization. Your job is to identify these and other competencies that may be unique to your role and seek out education, mentors, and an overall support system to become a continuous learner in those competencies essential to your success. The skills I address map to these core disciplines:

> ➢ Selling skills
> ➢ Technical knowledge
> ➢ People skills
> ➢ Executive acumen

Selling skills

Selling. Well, this seems like the most basic skill you should already possess. Presumably you've become very good at this to rise to your current position, but as with any competency, you have gaps. You may now have oversight for products and customers that are new to you. You now oversee a much broader spectrum of selling responsibility, whereas before you could focus solely on your specific area. Model a student's behavior. Shadow the expert salespeople. Meet the customers. Understand the nuances across your business and revisit those that have become second nature to you.

Be aware of incumbents who criticize you based on these gaps, and about the expertise you don't have yet. Be honest with these critics and demonstrate your commitment to learn and lead. You'll need everyone's confidence and support to get off to your best start.

Customers. If you are being promoted, you know your direct customers, though your perspective may be confined to the understanding you needed in order to make a sale and deliver your sales targets. You probably don't know customers that were the responsibility of others on your team. If you are new to your organization, unless you have come from a direct competitor, your specific customer knowledge is likely very limited.

In either case, you will need a much more expansive perspective about your customers. You need to elevate your understanding of your customers to a strategic level. You are no longer working to be a preferred supplier of products to the customer, you are striving to become a *strategic adviser*. A business consultant who can offer insights that support the success of your customer's overall business strategy.

While your team is functioning at the tactical level working on ways they can complete sales on a daily basis, you have to behave differently. You have to walk in the owner's shoes and understand how she wins in the marketplace. How does she make money? What challenges does she face as she tries to grow her business, or perhaps to simply survive against her competitors—competitors who may also be your customers?

This is very tricky business. Model your strategic curiosity about your customer's situation and set the proper example for your salespeople. Think about each customer as if you were consulting them on succeeding in the marketplace, whether or not they were buying your products.

We'll go into more detail on the customer relationship hierarchy in Chapter Five. For now, here's a brief visioning exercise. Think of your relationship with your best customer. Imagine them calling you for your counsel on a business dilemma outside the defined parameters of your relationship as customer and supplier. I'll bet that as you move down the list of customers, that likelihood will fade. Construct your reputation as a strategic adviser by stepping in that direction with all your customers.

<u>Sales Calls.</u> Finesse is essential when joining your people on sales calls. Be careful here. I've seen sales managers dominate the agenda in customer meetings and allow ego to take over. Often the result is that the sales rep doesn't get a chance to complete the presentation she prepared and the sale is not closed. Perhaps worse, the sales rep will avoid inviting the boss to future meetings, and the customer's perceived status as a prioritized customer to your company will be negatively impacted.

As leader, you must have strategic level conversations with the customer, but those should occur on the margins of a planned agenda by your salespeople. Speak to the owner or CEO before and after the meeting. Establish a relationship where you can break bread together or arrange for a separate one-on-one call to talk strategy. Be transparent with your salesperson about what you discussed. It is critical that you are supporting her and not undermining or overriding her.

Sales Cycle. Understanding your unique sales cycle takes on new importance now that you are leading the overall sales function. As an individual contributor, you had firsthand knowledge of your customers' buying cycles. You knew when they had budget dollars available, recognized the buying signals from their merchandising teams, and anticipated the cadence of contract negotiations. Instinctively, you understood what these and other factors meant to your ability to deliver sales.

As leader, you now sit at the intersection of plan execution and contingency management. First, listen to your salespeople, those who are closest to the customer. Second, know and develop your relationship with customers. You should be able to pick up the phone at any time and have a conversation with the corresponding leader at your customer's company to cut through the fog. Third, do your own independent research about your customer and question any red flags. This includes press, industry rumors, or insights from colleagues you have in common. Anything that has a potential impact on the sales cycle should go to the top of your must-know list. Seek the truth without delay and know the sales cycles of your business better than anyone.

To the degree that you can build a reputation of accurately assessing the sales flow, and guide your team on how to influence the cycle in your company's favor, you'll build your reputation as a credible leader of the sales function. Keeping things real is the key. Don't get caught in the optimism trap and tell your executive team what they want to hear about when sales will come in. No matter the pressure, give the facts as you see them, along with your plans to influence those outcomes and their timing.

Boundaries. As a salesperson you avoided the word "no" at all costs. Your existence was built around finding a way to say "yes," or at least, "Let me check with my manager and get back to you." Now you are the manager. You need to think very differently about these words.

Speed and simplicity in the sales function are the keys to your team performing and producing at a high level. You want your salesperson to project authority and empowerment when she is face to face with your customer. In order to achieve this, eliminate ambiguity when it comes to what is in bounds and out of bounds in response to your customers' requests.

I had a sales leader who liked to call these the guardrails. By defining the guardrails, we could handle 80 percent of the ad hoc requests from customers, and streamline our selling efforts. I appreciated that as a salesperson. I knew that I could address almost anything the customer threw at me, and I could build momentum by minimizing action items I needed to follow up on in order to complete a sale.

You are taking over a business that already has a rule book. There are rules about pricing, promotions, trade spending, terms, delivery, special orders, and many more transactional elements. Understand all of these, gather input and perspective on any you want to change, and build consensus and alignment around those changes. Clearly communicate the boundaries to your sales leaders and sales team, and make sure you have buy-in from everyone. Lastly, verify that these are being properly implemented in your team's customer interactions, and adjust any that are creating undue relationship conflicts.

Additionally, if you have been promoted or hired into your new role following the dismissal of the prior leader, there are bound to exist some lingering points of conflict between the sales team and that former leader. Look for the underlying problems that caused these conflicts. If the previous leader lost the loyalties of his team, there's a good chance the rules in place were incongruent with the needs of the customers and the voice of the sales team. Pay attention to these. There is likely an opportunity for you to fix something quickly and accelerate alignment and loyalty from your new team. If you came from the team you are now managing, you'll know what these issues are. If you are new to the team you'll need to surface them through your initial one-on-one conversations. Act promptly on the ones that are clearly affecting the morale of the team.

Technical knowledge

<u>Products</u>. Again, there are new dimensions to your requisite product knowledge when you become the leader. Knowing the technical specifications and application of all your products is still essential. And yes, you may have to expand that breadth if you now have oversight for business beyond your prior area of responsibility.

Now however, you have a portfolio interest in understanding how your products relate to each other and how they impact your ability to deliver sales results.

> ➢ How do customers make money with your products?
> ➢ How do they use one product to support another?
> ➢ What is the profitability mix and which products are your loss leaders?
> ➢ Where are the gaps in your product line?
> ➢ What product changes do you need to advocate for to your product and marketing teams?

It is inevitable that as you settle in as leader, over time, your level of knowledge on the products you sold as an individual contributor will fade. You've got a lot more on your plate now and you have to elevate your understanding of many topics, including your product knowledge. You must however maintain your credibility as a knowledge leader as it relates to your product line, even as you transform that knowledge to a portfolio perspective.

Work first to fill any technical knowledge gaps you have, then immerse yourself in understanding how your overall product line contributes to the success of your business. Also, watch out for the pure profit perspective in understanding which products to pursue, maintain, or drop. Unless you have a healthy understanding of how your customers make money with your products, you're likely to advocate for financially motivated changes in the portfolio that produce negative unintended consequences for your customers. Make any big changes on a pilot scale first, and be prepared to learn and adjust as you get customer response signals, and before you apply the changes more broadly.

Develop a small network of go-to experts who can educate you quickly on the latest trends and needs on the product development front. This network should consist of a savvy customer-facing person or two, as well as a key contact in your company's product development and product marketing functions. Include the person in your company who focuses on profitability from your finance department. It's important to have this person connected to the industry and customer factors when considering choices about adding or dropping products. Again, beware of the tendency to look at product portfolio decisions as purely mathematical or financial propositions.

Services. What are the value-added services your firm provides as part of doing business? As a direct sales rep, you focused on the essential services such as fulfillment, terms, credit, and other basics. Now you may need to become knowledgeable in services your company doesn't yet provide but perhaps your competition does. What are the trending services that are emerging in your industry? You need to have the pulse of these capabilities and become the primary advocate in your company for continuous optimization of the value-added services you provide to customers.

To access these emerging business requirements, connect to the leading industry associations and networks. In addition to developing an expert contact list, participate in panels and committees related to topics like customer analytics and insights, category management, regulatory initiatives, and other broad industry topics. Become expert across these topics and the thought leader to your customers from your company.

To be clear, your primary responsibility is to keep the trains running. You must have a keen sense of the performance of your sales operations through the eyes of your customers, and an internal network that you can quickly access and influence when things go awry. But now your role demands that you also pull your company in the direction of emerging trends. Leading edge customers are looking for the supplier that secures the strategic adviser space. Don't delay becoming immersed in your industry associations. Advocate that your company participate actively in these organizations. You have an obligation of service to your industry. Counter the tendency of those in your organization who want to cut participation because they look at membership as merely an expense, not easily tracked to sales and profits.

Application Knowledge. Your company has systems to help you manage your business. Customer Relationship Management (CRM) applications, trade management systems, budgeting and planning systems, order and fulfillment systems. When everyone is using the systems effectively, and when the systems themselves are performing, everything is fine. My experience is that is not always the case.

Most of the systems that you needed to understand and use as a client salesperson, are different to you now. You need to be assured that they are working properly, but you may no longer have as much hands-on interaction with them. Then, as enhancements are implemented and the users learn new features, you may actually find yourself in a situation where you don't know how to use them anymore. You don't even know how they work. This is not a good place to be as leader.

Challenge yourself in this area. Become an expert in the systems your people use, or your systems may take on the role of sales preventer rather than sales enabler. When you don't know how your CRM application is working, or how your people are using it, you don't know how effective it is in helping the sales process. If your trade management package is too complicated, your people will do everything they can to avoid using it and make deals that undermine the visibility you need.

For any system currently in place that touches your business, you need to have practical knowledge about how it works, what its role is in the selling process, and any gaps that need to be filled based on its limitations. Access the power users on your team who can train you and demonstrate how they use your systems. Spend time with the users who struggle with the systems so you can identify the reasons your systems may be slowing your people down. Your applications are only as effective as how well your most challenged user can utilize them.

Establish a strong relationship with your IT lead for each application. Make sure these tools are helping your business and recommend any changes you see necessary. Your portfolio of applications needs to complement, not compete, with each other. Make sure they serve you and you are not serving them. You can't do that unless you know what you're talking about from a technical standpoint.

People skills

<u>Hiring</u>. Among your most important responsibilities is hiring new salespeople or staff to support your growth. You may have open positions to fill as you assume your new role, or perhaps you're on a growth trajectory and need to add resources. In any event, you'll soon be hiring new talent for your team. Hiring employees is your most enduring legacy as a manager. The people you hire well impact your company for years to come. The people you hire poorly also impact you. Quickly. How do you become effective at hiring well?

As a hiring manager, you wear several hats. You are a project manager, managing an overall process and hiring team. You are a facilitator, guiding the development of the candidate screening process, formation of the interview panels, and the interview itself. You are the budget owner and lead negotiator, guiding the offer process. You are the business owner and lead decision maker, with overall responsibility for the selection of the best candidate. You're also the training manager, making sure the new employee you've selected gets off on the right foot.

Before it is time to hire a new employee, become familiar with established protocols and drive for any necessary changes.

> ➢ Do the position descriptions reflect your desired profiles of the roles on your team?
> ➢ Is the pre-screening process optimized?
> ➢ Does the company have a good track record of getting strong candidates to the interview table?

> ➤ Do interviews properly surface candidates' strengths and weaknesses?
> ➤ Are they conversations or quizzes?
> ➤ Is your post-interview process for evaluating candidates objective or subjective?
> ➤ Are all voices heard and have you established consistent criteria for comparing candidates?

These are all elements you need to assess and refine. You will be judged for years to come on the people you bring in. Your effectiveness in this area will have a lot to do with whether you rise or stall in your organization. Hiring requires your clear ownership. Understand the hiring philosophies of your Human Resource lead and your direct supervisor. You don't need to automatically adopt their approach, but you need to know their perspectives so you can influence them as necessary.

Listening. Of course you have to be a good listener. You're in sales. You listen for buying signals and red flags from your customer all the time. So why should you bother developing your listening skills further now?

The number of people you have to listen to just grew exponentially. There are your team members. If you oversee multiple teams you have to tune your ear to employees on each of those teams. Then there are your customers, which now include everyone's customers. Don't forget your functional colleagues across departments. Lastly there are senior leaders and external stakeholders. That's a lot to keep straight without your head spinning out of control.

Too much information is too much information, so you need to cut through noise and focus on what's essential to help you achieve the objectives you have committed to deliver. There are two areas where you can strengthen your listening muscles.

First, access a basic memory exercise course or application. There are plenty of good ones. These are essentially calisthenics for your mind. Make yourself better than anyone at remembering details, names, and meeting conversations. For example, I am not good at remembering names unless I hear them twice, or more. I always repeat a person's name when I meet them, and usually confirm that with them before we separate. On the other hand, I have a knack for remembering the conversation details from a meeting. I find that writing down detailed notes after a meeting helps my memory and clarifies my understanding of the discussion. I usually offer to make the first draft of notes after a meeting for this reason.

The second thing you can do to help your memory is to simply slow things down. Watch a top executive give an interview or answer audience questions and you'll see this. If they face a three-part question, they'll repeat what they heard for clarification, or even answer one part and then ask for the questioner to repeat the other parts. There is no fire. We have a tendency to want to answer quickly so we won't forget anything. When you are facing questions from any audience, take your time. Buy time by clarifying the question, asking a question, or just elaborating a bit on your responses. Avoid giving yes or no answers unless you must. When addressing senior executives, make sure you have the time you need so you can answer the way you want to answer. Control the pace and keep your head clear by using good listening techniques. There is formal training available for you to learn these specific skills, and practice is the best way to become adept at turning your listening skills into a powerful career asset.

Performance Management. If you are rising from within your organization, you have a client's perspective on the performance management process. Here again, you'll need to elevate your perspective so you can see that process from the manager's vantage point. Focus on two dimensions: process and style.

Process. Understand the cycle, cadence, and deadlines for completing your company's performance management reporting process. Share that overall schedule with your team members so they have the same visibility as you. You'll need to muster your best project management skills, and plan your calendar around deliverables expected from you. If you are managing a remote team, this means you may want to schedule review conversations well in advance of key deadlines. You really want to try to have face-to-face conversations with your employees at this time, to provide the best feedback and coaching you can. Meet your company's deadlines without rushing things at the end. Don't make your employees feel that you are not dedicating enough care to their careers by treating this like any other task or by rushing it.

Style. Develop your signature style of managing performance. Build your own tradition of managing your employees' career path with an empathetic interest in their long-term growth and success. Start by finding out who is doing this process well in your company. Who develops employees that are rising in the organization? Which teams seem to be most progressive in their thinking and in their strategy? Who is the leader that is not only boss, but also a thought leader and coach for her team? Seek that leader out and model her approach to performance management.

Another resource in developing your own style is your Human Resources generalist. An emerging trend in HR is to build department-specific teams that have a balance of people management skills along with strong business acumen, specific to the company's field of play. Who is that person in your company? If it isn't your assigned HR specialist, find out who that person is. Establish a relationship and ask that person to mentor you on how you can most effectively manage performance and develop your people to deliver real business objectives.

Firing. I'll go into greater detail about how to part ways with an employee in Chapter Six when we discuss managerial courage, but this is a reality you'll need to face as leader. Nobody likes terminating an employee. It can be an emotional situation for everyone involved. The fact is that it is a necessary skill for you if you are to help your company grow and succeed.

Let's discuss the basics. Understand the protocols in place at your company for terminating an employee.

➢ Do you have an at-will employee environment?
➢ Can employees be terminated for no cause and can they leave without notice?
➢ When terminating for cause, what are the prerequisite steps you must complete to try to correct performance prior to termination?
➢ Finally, who is involved and how is an employee notified when it's time to part company?

You may be taking over a leadership role where the team needs changes. Perhaps the prior leader dragged his feet on dealing with problem employees. It's also possible that everything is fine for now, and you won't have to deal with this process until later. In any event, this is an area where you'll want to lean heavily on your HR specialist. For legal protection, you need to follow your company's process very closely. Make sure someone who knows that process is guiding you every step of the way.

Lastly, don't get caught up in traps driven by rules of thumb. For example, some leaders subscribe to the belief that you should be changing out 10 percent of your team every year. Perhaps you are a new leader and have carte blanche to orchestrate a large team transformation by replacing employees. Regardless of how you arrived in your new role, treat terminations with a gentle hand. Make only the changes that your business strategies justify. Start with a mindset to develop employees to perform effectively. When it becomes clear to all that there is a poor fit, then make a change. Remember that the actions you take when terminating an employee will be noticed and remembered by your team members who remain.

Executive acumen

Planning. There are essentially three dimensions you'll need to master when it comes to strategic planning. You'll be in a continuous state of refinement in this area of expertise, but exercising good self-awareness and constructing your own planning philosophy is a must.

First, become familiar with the planning cadence in your company and master the mechanics of that planning.

> ➤ What is the planning calendar and when do key milestones occur?
> ➤ What tools are used for planning? Does your company use spreadsheets, a planning-specific application, or some combination of tools?
> ➤ Is the process collaborative or independent?

> ➢ Do plans cascade from the top down or build from the bottom up?

Chances are nobody is going to seek you out to explain all of this to you, so you'll need to dig for the basics about your company's planning process. Get trained on the tools before your planning cycle begins. This is so important. In my experience, trying to learn the tools while also thinking strategically about your plan can be a real challenge. Become your own project manager. Understand the calendar and begin your own process ahead of the key dates. Recognize key dependencies and the critical path toward on-time completion. Stay ahead of the major milestones and your peers so you are leading and not chasing either.

Second, develop your internal network of planning advisers. Start a continuous dialogue with key thinkers and influencers in your company's planning process. Ask questions.

> ➢ Who in your finance department has a hand in the roll up and report out of the financial plan?
> ➢ What is the early thinking about next year's promotional initiatives and new product launches?
> ➢ Are key initiatives from operations or technology functions that affect your business on track?
> ➢ Are there new initiatives coming at you that you're not aware of yet?

You need go to people with the knowledge and influence over any factors that affect your sales plan. Guide the way these impacts are communicated internally so others understand and accept the impacts to your sales plan.

Third, you need to be savvy and outcome-oriented as you build your plan. For starters, you should have a feel for how your team is performing against the current plan at all times. This means that you should dedicate time each week to review that performance and give your plan a reality check. Your plan should look out over multiple horizons. You need a quarterly plan, annual plan, and a three-year and ten-year plan. You may not be in your current role over all those horizons, but unless you have a sense for the long-term direction of your business, your plan will meander from year to year and you'll be chasing the latest attractive opportunities. This will harm your brand as a strategic leader in your company.

Another key to becoming a savvy planner is understanding the negotiation norms and nuances in your organization. At the end of your planning cycle, you want a plan that is achievable and challenging. Challenge your team to stretch and grow your business. You want to deliver compelling growth to your company without promising more than you can deliver. It's a balance.

Understand whether your executive team will accept your recommendation, challenge you to achieve more, or arbitrarily increase your targets at the end of your planning process. Build these contingencies into the development of your plan and don't get caught in a place where you risk losing the confidence of your team because you "accepted" an unachievable sales target. Unless you have this knowledge, you'll need to access it by establishing a trusted and well-informed mentor who can guide you in this dimension of the planning cycle. This person should be a regular sounding board to help you land on an optimal sales plan.

Financial Acumen. How does your company make money? As manager, it's time for you to think and act like an owner.

Understand your company's income statement, balance sheet, and other financial documents. Understand each line on these reports and your impact and contribution to each.

> ➤ How do your actions affect revenue and expense lines?
> ➤ How do allocated costs affect your profitability?
> ➤ Which metrics impact your ability to garner new resources to grow your team and your business?

Make decisions with these impacts in mind, based on your understanding of all these interdependencies.

If you've forgotten the things you learned in your college accounting and finance classes, it's time for a crash course. I recommend raising your hand up high and taking an outside financial refresher class, or getting proprietary financial training that your company offers. Many companies have developed excellent internal financial literacy courses, and you should definitely sign up for that now if offered. In addition, find your ally in the finance department, and establish the ability to go to that person for any questions or urgent tutoring you need. Don't be embarrassed about what you don't know in this area. This is definitely a need-to-know zone, and financial ignorance is one thing that can short-circuit your career progression.

One more note on financial acumen. Whether your company is publicly or privately held, the leaders at the top of your organization are thinking about your business from a financial perspective twenty-four/seven. Speak their language. Think of financial literacy as you would if you were learning a foreign language. According to Boaz Keysar, a psychologist at the University of Chicago, when mastering a new language, you must *think* in that language. [1] In my view, that is also true as you are building your financial acumen. Demonstrate that you are thinking about the business financially first. Your ability to master the financial elements of your business is one of the most important determinants of whether you ultimately rise from manager to executive. Be aggressive in your learning here, and convert your insights into actions that produce positive financial results.

<u>Organizational Design</u>. Chances are you will not be faced with needing to redesign your organization on day one. Even if a reorganization is called for, take time to understand the new team, the synergies in place, and the broken parts. Don't rush into making big changes to roles and people until you have that understanding.

Your first ninety days as new leader is an opportunity to review the landscape, and probably no bigger opportunity exists than during this time to understand how your team works.

> ➤ What is the structure of your organization and how well is it functioning?
> ➤ Is the structure a thoughtful design that takes into account the needs of your customers and the demands of the business?
> ➤ Is it simply a morphed construct from long ago with patches here and there put in place to solve the problems of the day?

You need to understand this quickly and begin work on a long-term design for your organization.

There may be no other responsibility that has the potential to send anxiety and shock waves through your team like your plans to reshape your team. Remember that your team members think of every action you take in terms of its impact on them personally first. Before they can appreciate the bigger picture, they need to understand how any changes you implement will affect them. Be aware of this and be as transparent as possible about your approach.

My learned approach to organizational change is to openly involve team members in the early brainstorming about what is working and what gaps exist as a result of the team structure. I encourage open dialogue and I like when team members discuss what the future structure might look like with each other. What form should the team take to capture the biggest opportunities? I believe the best ideas emerge when you get all of them into the space to consider and work them out. When I'm at least 50 percent confident that I have a coherent framework for a structural change, I'll bring in my manager and my Human Resource specialist to begin rounding out the rough edges and gain alignment. It's important for these constituents to know that you have general alignment from your organization before they are comfortable moving forward with a significant change.

A strong word of caution. Do not approach organizational change as a wizard behind a dark curtain. No matter how smart you think you are, or how much prior experience or perspective you think you have about what your team should look like, there are big risks if you keep it a secret. I've seen this. The changes you implement will feel abrupt to your team members. You'll spark intense water cooler talk and your team will become distracted from their essential responsibilities. In some cases, I've seen teams become immobilized because they are expecting the next shoe to drop. On them! They stop doing the right things in their daily work because they are afraid of making a critical mistake that will lead to them being bypassed for a key promotion, or worse, their dismissal.

Be open and inclusive with any major changes you are planning, and implement them carefully with the psyche of your team at the forefront of your actions.

Presentation and Public Speaking Skills. If you've gotten to this point on your career arc, you presumably have decent presentation skills. You've made countless presentations to customers. Despite your presentation experience, things are different now.

Your presentations to senior management should demonstrate that you are a competent business owner. Convince them that you have the credibility and expertise to manage and effect change in your business, and the capability to deliver the company's business objectives. You must instill confidence that your selection as leader was the right one, and that you are deserving of responsibility beyond your current role.

Resist the temptation to focus on being overly clever in your presentation habits. Understand how your audience digests information. Some do that visually, some by listening, some by taking information and reviewing it at a later time. Don't get caught in the trap of creating what you think are the most beautiful slides with subtle clues about what you are trying to communicate. Be bold and direct. Speak clearly and scan for comprehension. Ask questions to confirm understanding. If you are using charts or graphs, walk through them slowly. Don't assume your audience, who is seeing them for the first time, will understand them as you do after spending hours building them.

Nobody will comment after your presentation that slide fourteen was really interesting and changed their life. Just get your points across. I've had several presentations to the CEO and it never failed: that slide that I spent hours building to make my biggest point and was so proud of, went up on the screen when the CEO stepped out of the room to use the bathroom or make a call.

Public speaking proficiency is not about tricks or gimmicks, although there are concrete skills you need to acquire when it comes to delivering a great talk. Access your company's internal training or seek out outside training, like Toastmasters International or Dale Carnegie Training or similar providers, that focus on public speaking for executives. Get the tried and tested techniques to communicate effectively and with authority, and marry those with your own personal style. If you can deliver an effective fifteen-minute talk with no slides or props, and your audience can recall your main points, you'll have a great start on building the skills you need.

My experience is that when you're speaking to an internal audience, your credibility is the key ingredient in your speech. That's not a speaking technique. If you are establishing yourself as a credible leader, your audience will pay attention to what you have to say. If you haven't established your authenticity within your company, no fancy speaking skills are going to sustain your message beyond your allotted time on stage. I've seen credible speakers with poor skills soar with their audience. I've seen slick talkers fall flat. Believability always follows credibility.

If this is a new area for you to master, don't worry. This is one area where there is plenty of training available to help you improve. If you have a fear of public speaking, connect with someone you've seen who seems to be comfortable and effective speaking to large groups. You'll know that person when you see them speak. And remember, your audience wants you to succeed, not fail. They don't want to be uncomfortable either.

FUNCTIONAL COMPETENCE: APPLY IT

In order to effectively lead in the functional competences of selling, technical knowledge, people skills, and executive acumen, you must let go of self-deception. Let go of your instinct to cover up your blemishes, and seek new knowledge daringly. Knowing who you are, keeping your ego in check, and creating an environment where others can grow are essential principles to build broad functional competence. Follow these three principles to make sure you lead with your head and your heart.

Find out why you were hired

News flash. It's not because you were perfect for the job. Nobody is. You were better than the next best person. Do you know that story about being one of two people trying to outrun the bear? You only have to run faster than the other person, not the bear.

I've interviewed around a thousand candidates and hired a few hundred. I've often been asked by unsuccessful candidates why they were not hired. I've never been asked by a new hire why they were selected. The truth is, we all assume we were a perfect fit once we've been selected. Why would we have any questions about that? No need to dwell on the past, right?

There is a valuable secret here, however. Knowing exactly what the hiring team saw in you is incredibly instructive to you. You know how they perceived you. You know how well you communicated your strengths in written and verbal form. You know what skills and experience are most valued in your organization, and which may not be as important as you thought they were. At the same time, you need to ask about which abilities the hiring team did not see in you, or had questions about.

These may simply be things you didn't get a chance to talk about, or they may have seen legitimate red flags.

Exercise real self-awareness in this exercise. Your hiring panel will appreciate the inquiry, because they'll get a chance to know you a little better, get you started off on the right foot, and get some extra validation in their decision to bring you on board. You'll gain a crystal clear understanding of which skills you can leverage immediately because of your established capital, and which you should prioritize for development in your on-boarding learning process. Be honest with yourself and begin your new role with a clear assessment of where you stand.

Be a low ego learner

I chuckle when I hear a leader described as selfless or ego-less. The reality is that all of us are looking out for ourselves on a regular basis. There's nothing wrong with that. It's when that motivation clouds your empathy of people and situations that you run into trouble. When it comes to learning, it can be difficult for people who progress upward in organizations to be honest about what they don't understand. As leader, you are expected to be an expert across a wide range of topics. The people below you expect you to be a subject matter expert on any business topic that affects their daily world. If they can't answer a question, you are expected to have that answer. Those above you assume you have command over all issues relating to your business, that you know everyone in your industry, and you know where all the growth levers are and how to use them.

Get over that. Be transparent with everyone around you. Be open in asking questions and demonstrate your curiosity for learning. Develop the insight that comes from knowledge.

That's what your upper management expects of you. They want to know that you have the wisdom to exercise judgment when they're not around. Asking questions invites people in and tells them you count on their knowledge and their help. Open the door to mentors who can help you far beyond the current question you are struggling to answer. Make it clear that you are in it for the long haul, and you're not spending every moment figuring out how you can look like the smartest person in the room.

Create a culture of learning

Here's another secret that lies in plain sight. If you can identify a learning gap for yourself, there's a good chance that learning gap exists on your team as well. Look for opportunities to incorporate your education and development needs into your team's training plans. If you need a Finance 101 refresher training, your team probably does too. Explore whether a team-wide training on that topic is appropriate and learn together. As sponsor of the training, you'll have the opportunity to participate in the front end design work and success definition. Then, by actually participating in the learning you helped develop, you'll have turbocharged your own personal education.

There's one more reason for making learning a shared experience. Teams that train together develop common motivation, language, and shared experience in applying the new knowledge. My observation is that training completed together and then applied simultaneously is more effective and produces better results than training done independently or online. There's a benefit to human interaction as a part of your learning that should be leveraged when you have that opportunity.

Are these all the skills you need to know on your journey to compassionate leadership? No, of course not. They represent the foundational competencies you'll need to establish credibility. You don't necessarily have to be the most highly skilled in each, but understand what the best means for each. Lead your team toward that standard.

You're really on your way now. You have a strategic vision and you're developing the core abilities to master selling, customer relationships, and technology. You're thinking and behaving as an executive. You've got your team aligned to your vision. You're beginning to execute.

Are you ready to talk about producing actual results?

THREE

Productive Intent

"Do not mistake activity for achievement."
— *John Wooden*

Strategy and tangible skills. They mean little without results. Productive intent is not about being busy, looking busy, or multi-tasking. It is about working diligently, with the intent to create a concrete result, then producing that result. Consistently. Productive intent is the promise of strategy and execution. Effective leaders hold productive intent in their core. In their soul.

The Calm Between Storms

Vermont is a land of seasons. Ski season. Leaf-peeper season. Mud season. And the two weeks in the middle of July known as...Summer.

The serene scenes of the Green Mountain state draw visitors who want to experience the peacefulness of a fresh blanket of snow, an autumn explosion of color, or the lush greens in full bloom. Natives stay there for their entire lives. City slickers looking to slow down go there to turn their motors off. But these postcard images belie the tracks of the storms that created them, and the reality that another storm is just around the corner.

It's not just the weather that can get tumultuous. In the spring of 2003, our young management team was meeting at Green Mountain Coffee Roasters company headquarters in Waterbury, Vermont. Little did we know, but thunderheads were fast approaching.

Our management team had been formed following a storm of sorts a few months earlier, and was doing well so far as it found its footing guiding a national team of salespeople. I was the co-leader of that team, promoted from this group of managers when our leader had been abruptly let go. My colleague James ran sales operations and I led the sales force. These were battlefield promotions. Our business was falling fast and we had been tapped to turn it around. While I was now the leader of my former peers, I still felt very much like one of them. After five months, we had weathered that storm reasonably well and were beginning to turn the business around.

To call this team diverse would be a stretch. We were all middle-aged white guys who were married with a few kids. But we were different from each other in important ways. Different personalities and different styles. James was an expert at analytics. I complemented him well because I wasn't. But I seemed to have the skills suitable to lead a team of salespeople. My five Regional Managers were smart and experienced in the coffee business.

Day one of our three-day meeting went well. We seemed to be making all the right moves. No problems, no conflicts. We were about to wrap up for the day and head to dinner when our VP joined us.

His visit was brief and the task he handed us was clear. We were announcing a price increase the following week because our costs had suddenly spiked. He needed us to draft a customer communication and prepare the sales team with a talk track to deliver the news to our customers. This management team needed to have a conference call with the sales team the next morning. Have a nice day.

We had our marching orders. We found a comfortable conference room and ordered pizza.

Coffee is a commodity. Prices change all the time and our customers were aware of the fluctuations. They knew when to expect a price increase from their coffee roaster because they could see it coming. We had very good coffee buyers, and rarely changed prices because they hedged the market so effectively. Our customers liked that about us.

This situation was different. Commodity prices were stable, even falling a bit. Our costs had gone up because of our *own* doing. Our coffee department had changed the formulation of our core blends and sharply increased the costs. There was no turning back on that choice and we had to go get the difference from our customers.

This might take an hour, maybe ninety minutes. We would whiteboard the key talking points for the customer letter, embellish those for the sales team, build a PowerPoint deck and we'd be ready for the morning conference call. We'd probably have time to kick back at the hotel bar when we were done. I would facilitate the discussion and James would create the documents we needed from everyone's input.

We started. Seven of us in executive style chairs around a wooden conference table. White walls and numbing fluorescent lights. A lone tired whiteboard permanently stained with ideas from meetings past. One window gazed onto the now empty parking lot.

Mike spoke first. The longest-tenured among us, he had a strong sense of skepticism and only implemented decisions that passed through his fairness filter. "The cost increase wasn't our fault," he said. "Why do we have to take the heat with our customers?" Others agreed.

Gary, an idea man devoted to his people and his customers, and detail-oriented Matt, who led his team with a parent's temperament, both thought it was unfair to ask their team members to have such tough conversations with customers.

Barry was the newest manager, a coffee purist and affable teammate. He was always game for a challenge. But even he pointed out that customers knew coffee prices should be going down, not up. They would use it as an excuse to change to a new roaster.

Joe, a food industry veteran with big company experience, was a lieutenant who simply needed to know his orders so he could mobilize his team. He remained quiet. He just wanted us to get on with it. Thirty minutes passed.

We started again. Gary began brainstorming the list of points we should communicate to customers. Barry chimed in with a few more. Mike stopped the discussion, proclaimed how customers would object to each of the points, and reiterated that this whole thing was unfair. Joe was silent and visibly impatient. Matt debated the points that he felt would place his salespeople in a vulnerable position in their conversations with customers. We finally stumbled our way to a list of seven key talking points.

Another forty-five minutes had passed.

We began building our documents and our presentation deck. While James typed and projected onto the screen, Barry and I offered creative input. Colors? Charts or tables? Font? Grammar? Not much heard from Joe or Gary or Matt or Mike through this part.

Another forty-five minutes. I had now reached my outer estimate for allotted time.

It was time now to agree on roles for the conference call, timing for communicating to customers, and how we would monitor customer reaction. Now Matt sat up. As did Joe. It was time for decisions and implementation. These were their sweet spots.

Just then, Gary raised both hands into the heavy air and said, "Wait!" He told us we missed this point and that fact. We had to work those into our communication.

Mike pushed his chair back from the table and reminded us how unfair this whole thing was anyway. "We should just refuse to take a price increase," he said.

At this point Joe abruptly rose, sending his chair rolling back into the wall. "You're overthinking this," he told Gary. "Just tell the salespeople we're having a price increase and let them handle it."

"No," said Matt, who was accustomed to cushioning each fall for his people. "We have to prepare our salespeople with all the details. We can't leave anything to chance here."

Gary was also now out of his chair, feeling attacked. He and Joe faced off across the table. Close friends and colleagues despite their differing styles, they soon retreated and walked outside for some air and to stem what was quickly becoming an ugly escalation of tempers.

We were now two full hours into our task. And we were in a serious crisis.

This was ridiculous. There were obviously some tensions below the surface between us, but that didn't explain how this simple assignment had spun so wildly out of control. None of us wanted to diagnose the situation at that moment. We all agreed to bite our tongues, finish the work and accept its imperfections, and get the hell out of there.

Three hours and change after we started, we headed back to the hotel. The bar was closed, thankfully.

The next morning James and I led the conference call with our salespeople. The rest of the management team was silent, still stinging from the previous night's wounds. The sales team accepted our direction and embraced the tools. They took the message to their customers. In the following weeks, we received complaints from two customers and a thank you from another who appreciated the effort we made to explain the price increase to them. That second part was a first for me.

Obviously, something had worked. But something much bigger did not work. When it came to efficient and productive problem-solving, we were a broken management team.

James and I puzzled over what had happened for a few weeks. As we replayed our mental tapes something jumped out at us. An understanding of our collective and individual problem-solving styles was absent. James recalled a team problem-solving process rooted in Myers-Briggs (MBTI) thinking that he had been exposed to. It used an individual's MBTI profile to identify whether they were better at the defining the problem, developing options, choosing solutions, or the implementation phases of the problem-solving process.

We studied it. It helped us explain why Gary was continuously suggesting ideas and Joe was impatient to choose a solution. Why Matt wanted to get the action steps down so he could instruct his team. Why Mike wanted to redefine the problem. It explained many of the behaviors that made it seem like the team was functioning like an out of control popcorn machine.

We built this thinking into a tool that we named the Success Loop. We trained our management team on it. When we held meetings where we tackled problems and made team decisions, we hung charts on the wall so we could see each person's strongest contribution phase. We leaned on the person who was most suited to each phase. We self-managed ourselves not to pull others forward or backward in the process because of our own personal tendencies. We solved problems in good humor and never came close to a fistfight again.

For the four years this team remained intact, we never had another experience like the one during that otherwise tranquil Vermont Spring. Other challenges came and passed, but when it came to our problem-solving process, we were a model of productivity. We weathered each storm together.

Productive intent is about more than showing up and pushing through as leader. Bring practical skills and techniques to the process to arrive at your intended destination without undue delay. Goodwill and camaraderie alone will not take you there. Deliberate productive intent will.

PRODUCTIVE INTENT: RECOGNIZE IT

What Does It Mean to Be Productivity Minded?

There are many ways to describe leaders who are productivity minded. They are results-oriented or have a bias for action. They don't dwell on the problems they encounter. They tackle them head on. They always deliver 110 percent of what they are asked. If you want something done, go to that person.

There are also many ways to identify the person who acts too quickly.

> ➤ Ready, fire, aim.
> ➤ Shoot first and ask questions later.
> ➤ Let's just get moving and we'll figure the rest out later.
> ➤ Don't tell me about the labor, just show me the baby.
> ➤ Don't overthink the situation, just get out there and fix it.

A productive intent requires balance. It requires that you have a clear view of your desired outcome, and you're committed to making sure each step takes you along the most direct path toward that outcome. Know that time is of the essence, but don't take short cuts. Focus on your destination, yet understand that reaching it is only possible by taking many small steps. Take those steps as swiftly and as surely as you can. Keep your eye on the clock, on the destination, and on the team you've been chosen to lead. Make decisions that ensure that you all produce the outcome you are aiming for, and then move on to the next challenge with that same productive intent.

In some organizations, bias for action is management's way of saying, "Go faster. Stop thinking and just go." I believe I think better when I'm in motion. I like to move around when I'm trying to solve something or when I'm leading a conference call. So keep moving, yes, AND keep thinking. Remind those pushing you of the original plan and your progress and continuous learning about how best to achieve the intended results. Own your plan and your accountability to the plan, and articulate the implications of moving too quickly or without the proper information.

My colleague James introduced me to a book titled *Corps Business: The 30 Management Principles of the U.S. Marines*, by David H. Freeman. One of the principles is the 70 percent solution. Very simply, when the Marines head into a conflict, they gather all the available information that will help them prevail. When they believe they have 70 percent of that available information, they move ahead and engage. They continue to take in new information after they engage, incorporate that into their strategy, and adjust their course as needed. They are always on the move and they are not fazed by missteps.[2]

The United States Marines move forward when they've crossed their threshold of understanding about their situation. But they don't stop thinking. They keep gathering information as they are moving. They refine their steps as they go. The Marines have productive intent. When their mission is completed, they've achieved the best possible outcomes and they understand the entire picture more fully.

The productive leader understands how to expend her available energy on the activities that produce results. She thinks about abundance, not scarcity. She doesn't waste time managing information. She gets it flowing and acts upon the insights that emerge. All her energy is directed toward forward motion. None of it is spent on pulling on the reins of progress. Her intent is clear.

How can you move your team to the result you want to achieve in the most efficient and optimal manner? Whether conducting a thirty-minute conference call or working to secure a significant contract with a major customer, leaders with productive intent are always conscious of finding the most direct route to success, with as little wasted effort as possible, and with the interests of all involved in mind. Challenge others with empathy. Probe for issues. Prioritize. Gain agreement and move everyone ahead to the next space on the path.

In my little story about my meeting, it was obvious that I lacked productive intent on that day. I was behaving according to my flawed perception of the perfect leader. The leader who believed that good intentions and goodwill would carry the day over skilled facilitation of my team. Instead, I became the leader who alienated his closest team members by failing to appreciate individual problem-solving styles and recognizing the stress inherent in those differences. While I fortunately learned from my mistakes and recovered as a leader, on that day I was no leader. I was a problem.

There are six common scenarios I want to illustrate to help you understand how productive intent can come to life in your role as sales leader. These are typical situations from my career, ones you'll face on a regular basis. They include the various meetings you'll lead, planning cycles, sales calls, and special projects. Make yourself comfortable with recognizing opportunities to drive for the timely outcomes you want in these settings, and you'll find this competency to be one of the most enjoyable areas of strength in your repertoire.

The good news is that once you start to put this skill into practice, you'll find yourself behaving this way instinctively. And by creating a productivity culture, others will emulate your behavior and you'll have allies to keep you and your team on time and on task.

One-to-one meetings and calls

This may be the most elementary function in your role as sales leader. You are the head coach. First and foremost, you are the guide for your team members as individuals. You are their sounding board, compass, counselor, and tactician in their daily quest to sell your products and satisfy your customers. You are their last refuge when they have a problem they cannot solve themselves. That's a huge responsibility. It's a regular opportunity for you to shine as a leader, and it's rife with challenges.

These conversations take place in many forms and venues. In the car before and after sales calls, at dinner during a sales meeting, at a trade show when you're wearing your feet out in your booth. Your team member may simply want to pick up the phone and pick your brain about something as it shows up as a problem for him to solve. All of these are opportunities for you to guide your salesperson, to learn something new, and to synthesize your collective understanding about how your business is functioning across your team. Be open and ready to handle all of these conversations efficiently.

I recommend that you schedule a regular conversation with each of your people. Weekly thirty-minute one-to-one calls worked well for me. On this call, your salesperson sets the agenda and sends it to you ahead of the call. Just a few bullet points on the topics she wants to discuss. She should also tell you what she needs from you on each topic. Does she need your coaching? Your expertise and guidance? Is she looking for an approval for a deal? Is she simply informing you about an action she has taken or will take? It should be simple. If it takes her more than ten minutes to build this agenda and send it to you, it's too complicated.

Your salesperson runs the call. She works through her agenda. You know exactly what is coming, and more importantly, you know precisely what she needs from you on that topic. You don't volunteer new topics or hijack her agenda with something that is more important to you. This is her call. If there is time at the end, you can introduce new topics, but you keep the call to thirty minutes. I used to schedule these in succession with my team members so we stayed on task during the call. If there were topics that we needed to discuss further, we would schedule another call on that topic only.

If you adopt this approach to your one-to-one calls and stick to it, an interesting thing happens. Both people become committed to the rhythm of the conversation. Both understand the need and value of covering the topics efficiently. Both have productive intent. When the conversation is completed, the salesperson feels like she's been heard. There is a sense of accomplishment. Week after week, she understands that she can clear things off her plate. Problems don't tend to pile up and create undue stress. She understands that when a challenge shows up, it will only be a day or two before she'll be on the phone with you to discuss it. There are fewer and fewer fire drills.

Another cool thing that can happen is that *all* of your conversations become more efficient. Even the ad hoc ones. You can both call a time out when you're casually discussing a topic to get to the essence of that topic. You've developed a currency of efficiency in your relationship that you both value. Establish this across your team and get buy-in on how it can make you more productive. You'll be amazed how this little change can help you and your team go faster and sell more effectively.

Conference calls and web conferencing

Conference calls and web-based meetings are almost certainly a big part of your life as a leader now. If you are managing a regional or national team, you've got to use these tools to keep you and your team informed about a wide variety of topics.

Here are some basic best practices to make these more productive.

Treat each conference call like a face to face meeting. Build and distribute an agenda prior to the call. Be clear about your objectives, what you expect everyone to prepare beforehand, and the participation you expect. If you are leading and facilitating the call, plan on the questions you'll ask and set the expectation that each person may be asked to contribute. Guard against team members mailing it in. Understand the cost of a conference call in terms of the time value of your participants and the opportunity cost of everyone not working on sales-generating activities. Don't have calls because they're easy to schedule.

When you've achieved your objectives, end the call. If you're not achieving your objectives, reexamine your preparation and make sure you are setting yourself and your team up for success. Productive intent pursues a result. Nobody likes to be on calls that go on endlessly and feel like a waste of time. If they are valuable and there is a predictable tangible result for everyone and not just you, you'll get better participation.

For web conferencing, the same principles apply, plus a few more. Typically, a web conference is used to inform the team about something. It is a training presentation, to report financial results, or to take the team through a new key initiative or an update on a current one. You need the visual tool to provide richer context or to illustrate details more thoroughly. There are lots of tips on how to do this well, but here are a few that I've found to be indispensable:

1. **Distribute your presentation before the meeting** so your people can read and digest the information. I've seen too many examples of presenters who tweak

elaborate presentations up until the minute before the web conference, then take their team through complicated information. When they ask for reaction, they hear the sound of crickets. It's too hard and too risky for an individual to give a meaningful reaction or feedback to something they have to digest in thirty seconds. Give them the information in advance of the meeting and be clear about the type of feedback you're seeking.

2. **Show yourself using the video function.** It is tempting for your audience to do other things during your meeting in our multi-tasking world. Broadcast your image as you are delivering your materials. I've found, as presenter and as an audience member, that people are drawn to the visual image of the presenter. The body language and pseudo eye contact add valuable context. They are more likely to stay engaged and ask questions.

3. **Do not video your audience unless there is a clear reason to do so.** First, nobody wants to show what they look like to the whole group. If they are remote salespeople and are working in the office that day, they are probably having a casual day. They don't want to be on display in their baseball cap and T-shirt. Second, the distraction of having multiple images on the screen will ensure that nobody hears a word you're telling them. They are all looking to see what everyone else looks like that day. Leave everyone alone to focus on your message.

4. **When possible, appoint a co-facilitator** to help you with your meeting. This person can monitor chat, run polls, and address any connection issues. Give this person a speaking role, even if that is only to change up the voice that people are hearing. Nobody wants to listen to you for sixty minutes straight. Even if the role of your co-facilitator is largely administrative, the variety of voices will create a more dynamic feel for your audience and keep them engaged.

These tactics are basic but essential. Stick to them and repeat them consistently each time you hold one of these remote meetings. Get your team into a rhythm of productivity when you call them together and set the expectation that you're all there to reach a set of objectives and then disperse and get back to your work. Meet as much as you need to and no more. Meetings are expensive in many ways. Get the real value you need out of them and move on.

Live meetings

Your face to face meetings, no matter the scale, are your opportunity to establish your command as leader. All eyes are upon you. There are few settings where others are as fully tuned into who you are and how you behave. Take advantage of these opportunities.

Different types of meetings require different approaches, though all require you to take a deliberate approach to achieve your objectives efficiently.

The most common live meeting you'll lead is a staff meeting or a regularly scheduled meeting with your managers or your full team. These are variations of the conference call and web conference. You need an agenda, pre-work assignments, expectations about participation, and a clear set of objectives. If you are delivering material yourself or leading segments, you should have a person whose sole job is facilitation. This person keeps you on topic and on time. You may need another person to capture notes and assign follow up tasks. It is the rare person who can manage all of these activities along with delivering content and guiding discussion. Build your efficiency team for these types of meetings, either as permanent roles or assign them on a rotating basis.

The other common type of live meeting is more like an event. These may be presentations at conferences, sales meetings, or presentations to senior management or other departments. These are not meetings you lead, but settings where you need to present information coherently, confidently, and persuasively. Again, your moment to present your content is an important one. The impression you leave will last and live in discussions about the meeting long after your ten minutes presenting are over. Preparation is the key. Of course you must use good presentation skills, and as we discussed in Chapter Two, you can learn and practice these from a variety of sources.

In addition to becoming skilled in your delivery, you need a few extra ingredients to elevate this from a good talk into a productive pitch.

1. **Practice your talk in front of a mirror.** Many skip this simple preparation step. Watch yourself deliver and tweak your talk based on your own visual and auditory reaction to it. By physically practicing, you build muscle memory that will make your live delivery flow much more smoothly.

2. **Keep your ear to the ground** to listen to discussions and late developments leading up to your delivery. That talk you said was finished forty-eight hours before your scheduled time might be obsolete by the time you hit the stage. Identify any parts of your speech that are contradictory to emerging trends, shifting strategies, or even hallway chatter. Don't get stuck in a rigid speech because you weren't paying attention to the fast changing landscape around you.

3. **Get a few allies on your side.** You need extra eyes on your most important constituents. Ask a few close colleagues to read the reactions of key people you are trying to influence. Does a senior leader you are depending on for support show uneasy body language? Did the CEO go to the bathroom during your most important point? Get somebody to watch for critical success signals and get to those people before you get back on an airplane to go home. Make sure your most important points are heard and clarified so you can achieve your original objectives.

I treated live meetings like a championship game. I prepared my best, managed my blood sugar and got my sleep, and followed through on my performance before and after my presentations. Show your colleagues how much you value them by demonstrating your productive intent when you are on the main stage.

Customer account plans

For many salespeople, the notion of customer account planning as a productivity opportunity is an oxymoron. A customer account plan is more like a homework assignment from the manager to make sure they have a "gotcha" document when customer purchases are not growing fast enough. The salesperson knows intuitively what they want to sell their customer. *What's the point in wasting time writing all that down?* Consequently, the plan becomes a form the salesperson fills out herself with data and narrative that she thinks the boss will want to see. After all, these things never get pulled out of the file anyway, right?

No, not right. The customer account plan has the potential to be the single most powerful tool in productive selling and customer relationship building. It is the opportunity to collaborate with the customer and to be intentional about the customer's business during the coming year and beyond. However, if the customer is not co-authoring the plan with your salesperson, it is a waste of time. It's a meaningless homework assignment. Your salesperson must plan their business with the only person who can actually make that plan a reality, and keep the plan alive with that person throughout the year.

There are many methodologies and forms that the customer plan can take, from Miller Heiman (MHIGlobal) frameworks to proprietary models your company may have developed. No matter the approach behind the planning discipline, four elements must be present in order for your customer plans to work. That's productive intent.

1. **Understand the relationship.** As we discussed in Chapter Two, plans must reflect the true hierarchy of the customer relationship as understood by your company and the customer. Is the relationship viewed as transactional, is your company a valued supplier, or are you considered a strategic adviser who consults

with your customer on the entire category or overall business, not just your products? Gain alignment with your customer on the nature of the relationship so you can determine the depth of joint planning you'll do. If your customer only wants to order your products and pay your invoices, you're in no position to give advice on their overall growth strategy.

2. **Tie back to planning systems.** Whatever tool you use for joint planning must tie back to your systems and your customer's systems. Whether you are able to fully integrate your forms or simply keep them alive and retrievable within your respective customer and supplier relationship management systems, they must be readily available to support your plan. You and your customer need to be able to measure the results against your intended actions. If you committed to running four promotions per year, your internal system needs to prompt you quarterly to run them. If your customer committed to six days in the field working with his reps, he needs that to surface in his systems so it hits the calendar. Successful plans don't get lost in the file drawers.

3. **Align with your key metrics.** Your plan deliverables need to map to your company metrics. If you are measured against revenue, or units, or market share, then your customer plan needs to have those targets clearly stated. Don't waste time building an activity plan with your customer and hope that activity will result in the tangible results you're being held accountable to deliver. Make the plan as real as possible and make sure the customer understands your specific outcome needs.

4. **Align with the customer's key metrics.** Make sure the plan also reflects your customer's key metrics. Are they interested in major account growth, customer count and market share, or category leadership measures? If the planning process is only about increasing their purchases from you and hitting your targets, that's a big problem. Even if you achieve your plan, you may have a customer with a warehouse full of your products that she can't sell. That means next year's sales will be impacted, and your customer will lose trust in you as a strategic partner. Get clear on the business outcomes the customer is trying to achieve and make sure your plan maps cleanly to those outcomes.

Genuine and effective customer planning is a key productivity tool for you as leader. Establish this competency on your team to secure significant leverage with your customers. The heavy lifting you do at the start of the year will guide your success and help you reach your team's goals.

Sales calls

Let me guess. Here's how your salespeople think about a sales call. Thirty minutes long. You pitch your features and benefits to a buyer, or worse yet, to a small army of buyers. It's a chess game. You're trying to figure out what your buyer is thinking that she's not telling you. If you smile enough and only sweat on the inside, you have a chance of closing the deal. If she feels sorry enough for you, that is.

Shift this paradigm with your team. The sales call itself is really a small element to the selling process between your salesperson and her customer. If you instill with your team that this is a process, and not an event, the relationship balance she will pursue will empower her and change your customer's perception of your salesperson and your company.

I'm a big advocate of having at least two people from my team present at any customer sales call that is bigger than a maintenance visit. Two sets of eyes and ears ensure that you won't miss or misinterpret important information and signals from your customer. Some people think this is expensive, but it is no more expensive than making three sales calls instead of one because your salesperson and the customer are not on the same page. There are a few basic ingredients you need to establish with your team in order to produce sales consistently and predictably in these joint selling situations.

1. **Agenda.** You need an agenda for the sales call. This isn't what your salesperson hopes to achieve. *It's what your salesperson and the customer agree to achieve.* That means they need to have a planning meeting before the call, or at least correspond and agree to the agenda before the meeting. This accomplishes two things. It sets the amount of time you need for the meeting so you can complete the agenda topics. It provides a clear understanding of when the meeting is finished because you will have completed the whole agenda. There is no awkward silence or abrupt notification from the customer that you're out of time.

2. **Practice.** Next, for your team that is attending the call, you need to develop your content and rehearse your delivery. That's right, I'm talking about practice. Each person has to understand their role and how the material will be delivered. Where will questions be inserted? Who asks them? Who will be taking notes during

another person's speaking time? What objections and tough questions can be expected? Athletes practice ten times as much as they play in actual games. It amazes me how little salespeople practice before they are face to face with the customer. Make your practice perfect.

3. **Choreography.** On the day of the call, follow this cadence to execute the call. Before the meeting, you need a pre-game huddle. Coffee or breakfast before the call with your team. Review your plan again. Is there any new information to incorporate? Make sure your team is clear on the roles and on the outcomes you want to achieve. Calm any nervousness with humor or just by assuring folks that you've got their backs if anything goes wrong. During the call, put the agenda on the table, physically. Confirm that you'll follow it as agreed and be flexible enough to adapt to changes the customer wants to make. Then proceed with your meeting and secure the outcomes you came to achieve. Use your best practices for effective and efficient meeting management. That's all a sales call is.

After the meeting, you need a post-game huddle. Don't disperse and agree to debrief later. Share your observations and agree on commitments while it is still fresh in everyone's minds. One of my colleagues loved to start these conversations by asking everyone what they learned during the meeting. Share what you heard and pay attention to everyone else's observations to identify things you missed. Then agree on follow up actions and be on your way.

4. **Follow up.** The fourth and final step, which your salesperson should complete within forty-eight hours, is to synthesize all the notes and follow up items from your team and share those with her customer for confirmation. She might even want to have one more call to make sure the agreement is perfectly clear. Countless customer relationships are strained every day from perceived agreements that are not properly confirmed with the customer following the meeting. Chances are that the customer isn't having the before and after meetings like your team. They're not going to the same lengths to become crystal clear on the things you agreed to do. This is where you close the sale. Unless your business is extremely straightforward and you sign orders with your customer in person, your salesperson must complete this step to confirm your customer's commitment to buy your products. Completing this step will distinguish her and your company from your customer's many other suppliers.

Your sales process is unique to your business. Products that vary in complexity, sales to distributors and end users, and sales that are one-time versus repeating, will all affect the nature and duration of that process. Following this simple cadence, however, will give your team the best chance to win consistently in the marketplace, and enable you to create a sales team that sells with integrity and intention.

Special projects

Beyond your core selling focus, you'll face a number of other situations where you'll either lead or participate in processes that need a productivity champion. Whether it is during your longer-horizon business planning cycle, budgeting process, or ad hoc projects and key organizational initiatives, you must be the person who drives for outcomes that are on time and on target.

Project teams can be funny things. The leader may bring productive intent to the project. He has an outcome in mind and motivation to get there. But often the team is comprised of diverse members. Each has expertise in a particular area. Collectively the team represents the necessary combination of functional knowledge. The desire to succeed is another question. Besides the leader, this is nobody's top priority. They spend most of their time thinking about their regular problems. You must stand above that tendency.

Be the voice that helps keep everyone on track. Understand personalities and styles in each group. *Who in your group tends to brainstorm endlessly, even after the team has aligned around a decision? Is there another person who is only focused on implementation, who grows impatient with the work required before a decision is made? When are certain people active or quiet?* It may not be your owned initiative, but as a productivity minded leader, stay on guard for dynamics like these that can pull the train off the tracks. Get it to the station in one piece and build your brand as the leader who is driving the organization to complete work effectively and efficiently.

Workflow management systems and behavioral management tools and training can help you with effectiveness and efficiency. Pick one of each and apply the principles in a way that fits your own style and your company's culture. It isn't so important which ones you select as it is that you are acutely tuned to the pulse of your team and organization, and you're advocating for productivity at every turn as leader.

PRODUCTIVE INTENT: APPLY IT

A few words of guidance and caution when it comes to leading with a mindset of productivity. You are not driving a chariot. Productivity doesn't mean pushing the people around you right up to their breaking point, then easing off just a bit. It doesn't mean putting pressure on your team without providing an outlet for that pressure so you can keep all the gauges out of the red.

Your people already know the need to keep moving forward. Reminding them of that when a deadline approaches adds stress, not momentum. Take the time to apply these supportive behaviors to allow your team to solve problems, assess their own progress, or simply pause.

Understand the problem-solving styles of your people

I began this chapter with a story. On a fall evening, a group of managers and their leader met to craft a routine communication about an impending price increase. That meeting ended in near physical confrontation and hard feelings among the participants. Why did that happen? Why had seven people who had been otherwise friendly and even chummy with each other devolve into an angry group?

Everyone in the room had a unique style when it came to problem-solving and handling stress. Based on their personality style, each person was stronger in one problem-solving step than another. Being productive requires technique and intention, not just will alone. Know yourself. Know your team. Know where you are in your problem-solving process. Conduct your orchestra with that enlightened insight and your team will make beautiful music.

Bias for action doesn't mean stop thinking

This is a trendy phrase uttered by senior leaders these days. Everyone below them in the organization must have a bias for action. Beware of this phrase.

For instance, you'll face pressure from your company to not only deliver your plan, but to accelerate the sales and revenue your company derives from your portion of the business. Be very careful here.

Any sales you accelerate now will likely draw down sales you are counting on in the future. If you sell products to distributors, simply accelerating sales to those distributors doesn't guarantee that they'll be able to sell your products any faster to their customers. Now they have a full warehouse. Your team now has to help them sell those products and this takes their eyes off the ball in terms of your original plan. You make your senior leadership team happy this quarter, but you'll probably get the same request next quarter. Eventually the well runs dry and your perceived ability to run a productive sales organization is in big trouble.

Play it straight. When it's time to fill a gap, be honest with your company's leadership team. Don't poison the well this quarter. You'll still need fresh water, and fresh sales, next quarter.

Act with a bias for acting *smartly* and *swiftly*. In the words of legendary UCLA coach John Wooden, "Be quick, but don't hurry."[3]

Productivity sometimes means you must stand still

Don't mistake movement for productivity. Having a calendar where you are double-booked or have back to back meetings scheduled all day every day will make you reactive, not productive. It will impede your ability to exercise sound judgment, which we'll talk about in the next chapter.

Your day and your week should have gaps. I've seen too many leaders allow their calendars to become filled by calling meetings or accepting meetings that are not tightly aligned with their obligations to their strategic plan. I've seen leaders spend every week on an airplane with the mistaken assumption that they are being as productive as they can be. Don't fall into this trap.

Leadership is not a competition to see who can be the most miserable because they have a schedule that is out of control. Don't accept meetings that aren't aligned with your top priorities. Don't hop on airplanes because you think it will show what a dedicated leader you are. Work smarter.

Maintaining productive intent in your leadership style is an essential building block to your success. Understanding everything you are committed to at any given time is the only way you can exercise sound judgment to accept or reject the steady flow of new demands that come your way.

Now you're firmly in command of your schedule, your execution skills, and you're clear on your intended outcomes. The results will surely come for you now, right?

Success is not a linear equation. You don't run in a straight line toward the tape. Your leadership journey passes through a garden of choices. Its time for you to focus on what it means to demonstrate sound judgment in your journey toward compassionate leadership.

FOUR

Sound Judgment

"If Passion drives, let Reason hold the Reins."
— Benjamin Franklin

Strategy, execution, results. Repeat. Leadership success sounds simple, but it isn't. Variables, speed bumps, and crises litter your path. Take on each thoughtfully and assertively as you chart your team's course. Your decisions create your leadership brand.

There are no shortcuts.

Be Careful What You Wish For

On a fall day in Las Vegas in 2000, I got a call that would set my life on a course I had long hoped for. I never anticipated the surge of emotions that would accompany the first step on that journey. Or how I would manage them without collapsing beneath their weight. I was about to learn my most vivid lessons about sound judgment.

I was a Regional Manager, representing our company at a large trade show for the convenience store industry. Lots of great people work in this business, so by no means is the next statement meant to disparage any of them. But a convenience store trade show is a lot like the circus without the elephants. There is a wide variety of things going on. The major categories represented at the show were alcohol, tobacco, and pornography. The means the companies used to promote their products were, let's say, entertaining. In this environment, my colleagues and I staffed a booth and stayed focused on trying to write business with new coffee customers. We had a great time doing that, sore feet and all.

Outside the Las Vegas bubble, there was a tempest brewing in our company. Our National Sales Manager, my boss, was losing his grip on his role as leader. His productivity initiatives had missed the mark of what was actually required to drive business. Salespeople filled out detailed activity reports each week to demonstrate how hard they were working. Once people realized that these reports were simply stacking up without any real review process or diagnostics about how to use them to close business, they became filled with more and more fictitious data. The leader lost credibility with the team and the team lost confidence in its leader.

Senior leadership, once impressed with his initiative, didn't see the results they had hoped for. Our business was declining by double digits. On one Saturday a month prior, an anonymous letter had arrived in everyone's mailbox explaining that it was time for a change. Mutiny was imminent. I've never seen anything like it. I wasn't sure how it was going to end, but we were working in a contaminated environment. It was only a matter of time before things would start coming apart.

Back to Las Vegas, or, as a friend of mine had coined it, the city where nothing is real. At least not on the strip. Late morning on Monday of that week, while I was getting myself psyched up to head from my hotel back to the trade show, I received a call from our VP of Sales and Marketing.

My boss had been fired. Management had finally realized that the situation could not be resolved and new leadership was required to stabilize things. I was asked to co-lead the national team with my colleague James Jennings, who was managing Applied Insights. James and I had worked together on some projects, but we didn't know each other very well. My VP was clear, this was only a temporary arrangement until we could find a suitable permanent leader. I said yes, of course, I'll step up to this challenge. I hung up the phone and stared at the wall in my hotel room. Oh, my God. Now what?

Excitement, panic, fulfillment, inadequacy. The noise in my head was deafening.

I had competed with my now former boss two years earlier for the position he held. He was the leading external candidate and I was the leading internal candidate. We were both strong options and presented contrasting visions for what we wanted to accomplish as National Sales Manager. He got the job. I went back to my role as Regional Manager. I was wounded. It took several months before I could put it all behind me and get back to my career game plan of staying positive and performing.

I had made a positive impression during that process and continued to impress management up until this day. When the shoes started dropping and senior leadership looked around, I was their clear choice to stabilize things. When a permanent leader was in place we'd be no worse off than we were at that moment. It felt like an 80 percent endorsement of me as a leader, but it was better than nothing. And it was the door opening I was hoping for.

My mind raced with questions. What kind of leader did I need to be under the circumstances? What did I need to do first? Now that I was in charge of the whole team, did I need to change my approach? How would my peers react to me now as their boss? What about James? Co-leaders? Exactly how was that supposed to work? What about my existing team? Did I need to tell them? Did they already know? And finally, did I still need to go over to the circus, I mean, trade show?

The first decision I made was not to go to the trade show. Sound judgment in action. There, that was easy. It's great to be in charge and not have to check with anybody before making a decision, I thought. Later that afternoon, James and I joined a conference call where our VP informed our now former peers of the change. There were audible gasps on the phone. I'm not sure whether those were because our boss was fired or because Jim and James were in charge. We made arrangements to have our own conference call the next day so we could regroup and address the broader team.

Following the call with our VP, James and I talked to each other. We were both stunned, excited, and in a bit of a panic. After what had happened, what was the world we now faced? We thought about people first. We needed to talk with certain people quickly. People in the corporate office who had reported directly to our boss; other department heads who were working on projects or supporting our channel; customers and partners who had a direct line to our boss and needed assurances that their relationship with our company was secure. We divided up that work and aligned on messaging. More sound judgment. Check.

What we did next has stuck with both James and I as our proudest example of sound judgment during our moment of great stress. There were a thousand things to do. Instead of building a task list of the things we needed to start doing, we stopped. We cut through the fog and agreed that if we were going to work effectively together, we needed to agree on core principles that would guide our work, our decisions, and our actions. The principles became:

We win as a team.
The job of salespeople is to sell.
Make decisions as close to the customer as possible.
Speed and simplicity.

The principles were straightforward. They reflected the antithesis of where the team had drifted and problems we needed to overcome. But they were more than just that. They had a universal quality. They had the potential to be enduring.

We brought these principles to the team. We told them we didn't have all the answers, but we would exercise sound judgment in any situation with these principles in mind. We would reiterate them and prominently display them at meetings. When we got stuck, we'd go back to them and start over.

Everyone bought in. We knew we would start winning, and we did. Our business that was in double-digit decline turned into a double-digit growth business in eighteen months. We delivered twenty consecutive quarters of positive year over year growth. The principles—our centerpiece of sound judgment—worked.

After one year I assumed sole leadership for the business, and James and I remained close strategic partners in its success. We both describe these years as the most professionally satisfying period of our respective careers. It all started because we stepped out of the fog and exercised sound judgment in a chaotic moment. Together.

Leaders make judgments all the time. When you stand amongst your team, the eyes upon you assume your judgments will be sound. It's expected. But the ability to exercise sound judgment is not a given. It requires that you effectively quiet the noise amplified by the implications of each situation. This chapter is designed to help you find your internal calm and make better decisions on your path to becoming a compassionate leader.

SOUND JUDGMENT: RECOGNIZE IT

I Already Have Sound Judgment, Don't I?

Leaders who emerge and rise in organizations have a few things in common. They have probably performed well as an individual contributor. Their performance is objectively measurable. There is data to support their selection as the new leader. They may have a significant accomplishment or two that has captured the attention and appreciation of those in position to promote. That big customer win. The time they saved the day in a crisis. Perhaps they exude confidence and competence when on the stage. Their ability to articulate well when eyes are upon them set them apart from those who stutter or stumble.

Your process is harder to see than your results. How do you get from question to decision? What is going on in your head as you are trying to find your way? How clear is your thinking? Are you aware of all the factors and ramifications of the decision you face? Can you focus when everything is happening at once? What are your coping techniques? How do you function under pressure? Can you be counted on when senior leadership can't be there to help you decide?

The further you rise in the organization, the more acute questions about your sound judgment become. You have increasing responsibility over people, budgets, success, failure. You embody greater risk to the company.

There is an unspoken assumption that all employees rise to their level of incompetence. You are essentially a time bomb. At some point you'll be promoted into a role where you don't really know what you're doing. Then it may all unravel and you'll create a trail of destruction. The company is watching and will move quickly to replace you when it's your time. And it's just a matter of time.

I don't accept this assumption. That's not why you're reading this and it's not what you signed up for on your leadership journey. But what do you need to be thinking about so you don't fall into the trap that so many rising leaders face? How do you keep your career momentum? You need to be aware of a few basic survival principles to establish a foundation of sound judgment that you can carry with you.

Let's consider how your principles of sound judgment play in your ethics, your support networks, your relationships, and in the results you produce.

You need an ethical foundation

This goes without saying, but I'm saying it anyway. Your motives must be pure. Your ego must be low. Not zero, just low and in check. You think of others first. You have a long view of the decisions you make. You don't take any options off the table when you are considering a problem. There is no deal you have to have and there is no situation where no is not an option. If you make a bad call, own it. If your salesperson makes a bad call, make it a teaching moment and don't humiliate him or her. Don't run for cover or deflect blame.

These seem self-evident as characteristics of a modern compassionate leader, but things are different for you now. The consequences of the decisions you make have grown exponentially. When you exercised judgment as an individual contributor, the implications mostly affected you personally. There was minimal impact on others. Now you cast a longer shadow. You have stakeholders up, down, and sideways in your organization who are invested in the quality of your judgment. Understand and appreciate your new span of influence. Your decisions must be more thorough. You must consider more information, involve more people, and be more approachable. Others will drive you to decide quickly. Efficiently. You may feel the urgency to act quickly yourself. Continue to seek input, but stay out of decision-making quicksand. Maintain your ethical foundation and make your best decision in due time.

You need a support network

As an individual contributor, you rarely had to reach into the organization for technical, legal, or logistical expertise on the actions you took. Your company set you up with guardrails. You knew which options were in bounds and which were out of bounds. If you got into a situation that was outside the rails, you called on your manager for guidance. If you happened to overstep your bounds, you pleaded ignorance, asked for forgiveness, and it became a learning opportunity. Your judgment was sheltered. The risk of you creating a serious catastrophe was low.

Now however, you own more of the consequences of your judgment. You need help. You need a go-to person in your legal department to help you negotiate agreements with customers. A person in the finance department to make sure your deals are acceptable and don't cause undue problems with customers in other channels of business. You need technical assistance from IT and operations so that your team's promises to customers in terms of category management or fulfillment are feasible and don't knock some other process off balance for the company. The higher you go in your organization the less likely it is that you'll have one person above you to rely on for answers to all your questions. It will be different than it was when you were starting out and your manager had all the answers you needed.

Now sound judgment requires a broad and sturdy foundation. You can't go it alone anymore.

These critical people in your support network should not be ad hoc contacts that are available for your pop quizzes about what your team can and cannot do in a given situation. They need to be people who walk with you. Real relationships. People you spend time with, have lunch with, and socialize with when you can. Understand each other as people. Develop a mutual understanding of the challenges you face in your respective roles. Invite them to work with you and your team and shadow their work as well. Learn about each other. You are partners in the business, meeting at the intersection of your respective leverage points for your company. If they can't solve the questions that make you pause at that intersection, they can direct traffic for you so you can steer toward the person who can help.

Don't treat these people as different from you because you are in sales and they are not. At the same time, understand that as a salesperson, you may be the closest thing to a real alien that they know. Get to know each other and develop these partnerships. Their role is to validate as well as challenge your judgment. You can do the same for them. These can become some of the strongest personal relationships you'll know in your career. They will support your sound judgment as you rise professionally.

Your relationships—be present

Of course, right? Be attentive. Listen to your people describing the problem they face. Be aware of external factors. Ask questions. Don't rush to judgment.

The danger here is a little bit different from the prior techniques. To build sound judgment as you accumulate experience, you'll lay down a track record of decision-making. As your tenure lengthens, you'll begin to see situations that look a lot like those you tackled in the past. You'll say, "This is exactly like that negotiation we had with the other big distributor four years ago." All you need to do is pull the file and run the same plays. It's the same thing.

No, it isn't.

I've seen many managers fall into this trap. They go to their playbook. If it worked once it will work again. No need to puzzle over this situation. These are lazy leaders. In the interest of being efficient, they neglect to consider factors that are right in front of them.

Often, these leaders have already garnered the respect and confidence of their organization because of their past experience. Companies hire leaders because they have experience with a particular customer or class of customers. *If they can demonstrate their success with these customers, then they must know more than our existing people about how to handle the customers that are giving us trouble today. We can hire that leader and forget about those problems since he already knows the ropes.* When the leader faces the first situation where his judgment is needed, he directs the team to take option A because when he was at XYZ Company, that's what they did and it worked.

But it's not the same. There are different people involved. Different products. Different pricing and logistics and trade support. Different competition. I've seen these leaders lean too hard on their own playbook and fail. First they try to deflect blame onto the people executing the plan, who must not have done it properly. Energy spins onto an extreme focus on performance management, and collateral damage follows. Ultimately, none of the plays in their playbook work, and they wear out their welcome without delivering up to their originally perceived promise.

Stay in the moment. History does not repeat itself, no matter how familiar it looks to you. If you find yourself identifying a situation as exactly the same as that other time, stop. Make yourself ask questions about how it is different. Make others who were not involved in the prior problem give you their assessment. Don't stop thinking. Refer to your experience but don't open that playbook and simply run your favorite play. Look at your situation and devise a plan that will work now. Rely on your prior experience to remember the critical questions you asked in that previous situation. But don't take the short cut to the answers you came up with before. Those are only likely to be the right answers to the wrong questions.

Pay attention to results

The military does this. In the effort to institutionalize sound judgment and effective decision-making, the U.S. Army de- veloped a process called the after action review (AAR). This is a formal process after a mission or initiative is completed, designed to understand and document what happened. The AAR asks important questions about the process and specifically about the leader's actions. What were the intended results? What were the actual results? What were the events that occurred during the campaign that caused deviation from the plan? Were the reactions to the events appropriate? Were they effective?[4]

The critical output from the AAR is the potential learning that can be applied to future similar situations. How can other Army leaders apply the insights gained in the analysis to their own leadership challenges? How can the leaders sharpen their judgment? With an institution the size of the U.S. Army, it is critical to avoid repeat mistakes. Lives depend on the learning from shared experiences. Sound judgment isn't just a good management practice, it is an essential survival tool.

A lot depends on your sound judgment as well. The people around you, those you manage and those you collaborate with, need to know they can count on you in a crisis. They make a daily investment in their role and in their career to deliver their best effort and create positive results. They can't afford to have their leader guide them down dead end roads. They won't follow that leader for very long. But they will follow the leader that pays close attention to delivering results.

SOUND JUDGMENT: APPLY IT

What is the key to acquiring, possessing, and exercising sound judgment consistently? Is there a training course, a boot camp, something you can read? Should you just hang around with people who don't seem to get flustered when the storm hits?

Is it something you were born with, or worse yet, something you weren't born with?

Sound judgment, in my opinion, is most definitely a learned behavior. It is a developed way of thinking clearly through distraction and adversity. Sound judgment is developed over time and for most of us, acquired in the experience of setbacks. Sometimes major setbacks, sometimes minor. Occasionally they will be situations in which we observe and experience the behavior of others. But the keenest learning happens when we are the major character in the narrative. When a vivid outcome occurs because of an action we've taken, or failed to take.

Sharpening your judgment is a continuous process. Pay attention every moment. Develop a unique ability to be in the moment, to observe the moment, and to record the moment simultaneously. There is no delegation when it comes to this. You must own it. Here are three tips to keep you on track to building your tradition of sound judgment.

Accept your roles

You are the quarterback, the color analyst in the press box, and the journalist all at the same time. You play these roles in real time. Each time you face a decision, consider what will happen to you on the field of play if you run or pass. *How will the people watching you right now react to your decision and action? What will they say about you later when they are talking about what happened?* Your choices in any situation and at any time should consider these dynamics.

Be careful. Don't let these dimensions of influence cloud your thinking or rush your judgment. Don't fall into the trap of thinking you are serving three different masters. The decision you make should be compatible with each of these perspectives to get the call right. Ask yourself whether the decision you are making right now looks appropriate from all angles, and it will stand the test of time. And don't worry. You'll run many plays in the game. If you get a few wrong, you'll have a chance to learn from your experience and get the next one right. The accumulation of the decisions you make, popular or unpopular, construct your judgment architecture and help condition your team to use similar critical thinking techniques.

Set the pace when urgency arrives

Before you were in your leadership role you often had time to take a step back and reflect on a situation before you took action. Nobody was watching you. But now, everyone comes to you with urgency when they need to solve something.

As a leader, you'll feel what seems like an overwhelming urge to answer questions from all these constituents quickly. I've felt it. When the CEO asks you a question, you want to answer it. Right away. Your ability to promptly provide the correct answer is the true test of your mettle in his mind, isn't it? Your team members and your colleagues count on you to solve their problems quickly as well. You have to be quick and accurate on the draw, don't you?

No. We're talking about judgment, not speed. The best leaders I've seen in the middle of organizations are the ones who can defuse the urgency and avoid the urge to provide an immediate answer. They ask for clarification. They ask related questions. They articulate the factors that come to mind quickly and inform their counterparts that these and other factors must be considered to make the correct decision. They are not rattled by the apparent emergency. The fact that the other person is unsettled based on the unknown doesn't mean you have to adopt their same anxiety.

Remain flexible

Small decisions turn into actions. Actions turn into habits. Habits turn into culture. There is a rigidity that forms in organizations. Small decisions that you made a long time ago come back to haunt you. People faced with a current problem will remind you that you made a different decision two years ago. They will provide you with the documents you created to get your team aligned to your decision.

Plant the seeds of perspective when you are taking a position or prescribing an action today. Circumstances will be different in the future and you might need to change your position and bring your team along on that new course. You see this in the world of politics all the time. A politician running for office may evolve over time to believe in a new position on a controversial topic. Early in his political life, when he was running for state legislature, he held the opposite viewpoint. He is now running for the U.S. Senate. He has much more experience than he did in that first political run. He sees things differently. He would like to articulate his new heartfelt position on the issue now. But he is reminded of his starting viewpoint. That is what he said. How can he change his position? Doesn't that make him disingenuous? Can he be trusted? Won't he just change his mind again? How can I vote for him?

Be clear that today's decision matches the circumstances that are presented to you *today*. Be clear that what you decide now will *inform* future decisions, but will not *dictate* them. In the future, circumstances will change and a different decision may be more appropriate. Nonetheless, emphasize that the team must fully commit to this decision today and the actions required to carry it out. All future options must remain open so sound judgment can prevail.

Don't become enamored with your decisions or the documents you create to support them. Don't be too married to your awesome PowerPoint deck. I've seen too many examples of problems that are poorly addressed because of a rigid legacy created by leaders who are overly impressed with their prior judgment. Don't worry about contradicting decisions you made with less experience. That's how sound judgment grows in all of us.

The secret to sound judgment is that when another person hands their problem to you to solve, they have handed you the ball. You now control the ball. You decide what to do with it. You decide when to pass or shoot. Understand this when you receive the ball.

Remain calm. Even if you are swirling with confusion on the inside, keep a calm outer appearance. Remember, others are bringing this situation to you because you are their best hope, perhaps their last hope to solve it.

If you need to step away, call in help, or gain more information, it's up to you to insist on that. This is not a pop quiz on everything and anything you know about the business. Create the space to apply sound judgment in situations you face and build your credibility brand one deliberate step at a time.

Sound judgment is the skill that creates movement for you as a leader. Each decision moves you onto a new space on your career game board. And your decisions occur within a larger context than simply the current situation. In the next chapter, let's take a look at whether your decision-making is compatible with your long range focus.

FIVE

Long Range Focus

*"I tell you that as long as I can conceive something better
than myself I cannot be easy unless I am striving to bring
it into existence or clearing the way for it."*
– George Bernard Shaw

Where are you going? You are consistently producing results through skillful execution of coherent strategies.
You make the right calls in tough situations. But where is it
leading you? How far is your horizon for success?

Are you becoming? Or, are you just being?

This Brand Isn't for Everyone

I was in my early days at Green Mountain Coffee Roasters,
which by then was approaching fifteen years as a thriving
young company. As Area Sales Manager in the Mid-Atlantic
market, I was on the geographic frontier of the company's
reach and consumer awareness of the brand. I had less than
fifty wholesale customers at the start. But it was clear from
the beginning that there was something different happening.
There was a magic around this brand.

Immediately after completing my two-week training, I began meeting my customers. They were excited to see me. I arrived with a feeling of celebrity. There was a common element across almost all of these customers. The owner of the business, or the person that was responsible for selecting Green Mountain Coffee, told me about how they discovered the brand. These were not short stories. They were personal. Most involved a ski trip or family vacation in Vermont. They happened upon a remarkable cup of coffee that changed their life. They became emotionally attached to that cup, to our brand. When they returned home to run their business it became their top priority to source that coffee and provide their customers with the same experience they had remembered.

It was like they were telling me the story about how they fell in love. It was a story about a relationship. I was amazed at the similarities in the stories. They paralleled the story of our founder, Bob Stiller. Bob too had been on a ski trip in Vermont in 1981 and stopped into the original Green Mountain Coffee store in Waitsfield, Vermont. He had a cup of coffee that was the best he ever tasted. He met the owners, partnered with them, and eventually bought the company. He started what was to become one of the most exciting and compelling business stories in the past fifty years.

A cup of coffee changed Bob's life, as it would for those customers I met and for many others. I felt a tremendous responsibility to nurture the brand and not to harm it in any way. I was the custodian of something others had built. I had to continue their work and pass it down to those who would follow me in better condition than I had received it. I needed to focus on the long game.

In those days potential customers appeared in three different profiles. The first was the type that had made that journey to Vermont and fell in love as Bob and the early adopters did. The second type was the customer that didn't travel to Vermont, but had heard about the brand through word of mouth and were taken by the way customers spoke of their discovery. After I took them through a full immersion in the Green Mountain way, they wanted to hop on board and share our products with their customers too. The third type was different. They had become aware of Green Mountain Coffee because their competitor was selling it, and beating them in their marketplace. They were losing customers because of a product and a phenomenon that they didn't understand. They weren't interested in our story or heritage. All they understood was that they needed to have that product too so they could stop the leak in their business.

This third customer type was trouble. In many cases their businesses were not well run. Sometimes they were dirty. They didn't treat their customers as family, they treated them more like automated teller machines. They withdrew money in exchange for anything they could sell to them. They certainly didn't care about my brand. They expected me to plead for their business, and treated their suppliers with disdain. They believed it was my privilege to do business with them, no matter how they behaved.

My best customers, the true believers, gave me referrals. They told me about good prospects that I should talk to. They were sensitive when I added a new customer in their trading area, but if the new customer was quality-minded, they approved. The brand would be respected and the additional consumer awareness would help them. On the other hand, if I set up a Type 3 customer there was going to be a problem. If that customer wasn't up to their standard I was going to get a call, and an earful. It only took a few occurrences of setting up the wrong type of customer before I learned a valuable lesson.

Remember, I had been given a gift. It was a handmade gift, specially wrapped by others and given to me. A brand, a company, and a cup of coffee that created a unique personal bond with customers. There was a promise inherent in that relationship to do no harm and to nurture that relationship. To pass it down intact.

I decided that if each potential new customer would treat my brand in a manner that would make it likely for three more like-minded future prospects to become customers, they were qualified as a Green Mountain customer in my book. If they couldn't meet that standard I would refer them to another coffee company, because they would probably end up costing me customers in the long run.

This strategy helped me expand my customer base over my years as a direct salesperson and later as a leader in the organization. The values and discipline I adopted with a long range focus in mind helped build strong equity into the Green Mountain family of brands and created customers for life. I didn't make my decisions based on the potential personal rewards. I focused on building long-term value for my company and our customers.

Keeping a long range focus clarifies thinking. It allows you to set aside immediate gratification and see the lasting implications of your choices and actions. It counters the natural tendency toward expediency. Thinking about the condition that will exist long after your decision, when you are no longer present, takes fortitude. That's true whether you are building a future for your children, taking care of the planet, or setting a good example for your team. Compassionate leaders understand that they are just one in a series of leaders: those who have preceded them and those who will follow. Your legacy is not formed by becoming the most notable player along that continuum. It is in the enduring value you create and deliver to the next leader to follow you.

And let me dispel a myth. Short-term gains and long-term success are not tradeoffs. They are not mutually exclusive. You can achieve both. In fact, they are linked together. If you're clear on your long range focus, then stringing together short-term wins to arrive there will seem perfectly logical to you.

LONG RANGE FOCUS: RECOGNIZE IT

If you're not familiar with the Abilene Paradox, you need to be. This is an accepted example of how groupthink can undermine the ability of a group or team to function effectively, as a result of self-imposed silence about each person's true point of view.

On a hot, late summer afternoon in Texas, a family is trying to stay cool on the front porch. The father-in-law suggests that they all drive to Abilene to have dinner at the cafeteria. Amidst expressions of body language making it clear that nobody else shares his interest in the journey, each defers to the next to decide. "I don't care, it's up to you." "I'll go if you want to go." The family leaves the porch and heads off. When they return to their places on the porch a few hours later, there is a silence and their body language is even clearer. Everyone is perturbed. Then the father-in-law breaks the silence and says he didn't want to go to Abilene in the first place, and only went because everyone else wanted to go. One by one they all say the same thing. [5] Each is frustrated that this happened. *Why* did it happen?

When you are launching an initiative toward that big hairy audacious goal, as a friend of mine likes to call it, don't take your team to Abilene. Recognize that people will have a hard time reacting to the proposed goal initially. There is probably a lot of information to digest. They need to reconcile the new directive with everything else that is going on for them. They will definitely have questions. And while we constantly tell our people there are no dumb questions, everyone is terrified right now that the question they want to ask will qualify as one. Before you load everyone in the car and pat yourself on the back for getting your initiative out there, take a step back.

There's something worse than not achieving your big goal at the end of your initiative. Much worse. It's dragging your team along the way when they don't believe in your plan but are reluctant to tell you. This can be fatal to your credibility. The water cooler will be so busy your team members will need to take a number. It will result in enormous productivity loss and opportunity cost. It can stall your career and brand you as a manager who is no leader.

When you're launching a major initiative, your ability to surface questions and objections up front is paramount. Go slowly in your explanation and test for comprehension and alignment frequently. Identify the people in your organization who are likely to object. Those who have a regular parking space at the water cooler. Check with them in front of everyone to confirm that they are on board. Address any questions that surface from the room and follow up later to thoroughly answer the ones you can't answer immediately. Anticipate questions that are swirling around in people's minds and put those into the room yourself for discussion. Take no chances and don't end up on that front porch after your project has failed or after you've been replaced, only to find out nobody wanted to get in the car with you.

Abilene is a nice place, but don't go unless you're absolutely sure everyone wants to eat there.

It's important for you to establish appropriate reward systems, steer progress, ask provocative questions, and provide regular feedback on results. The following four techniques will help you become the mentor your team needs to guide the way for them.

Establish sensible incentive plans

I talked about the need for you to be adept in balancing the demands of today with your longer-term goals back in Chapter Two. So far, I've focused on that balance from a workflow management perspective, and the need to avoid putting too much emphasis on short or long-term objectives to the detriment of the other. Now I'm speaking about something different. I'm speaking about what you are becoming. About what your team, your organization are becoming. About what individuals you guide and influence are becoming and how you can help them flourish in their endeavors.

As you progress upward in management, you'll move from providing input to your incentive plans to authoring and owning those plans. It's important to understand your options in the reward systems you devise for your people. Every incentive plan, commission schedule, and bonus structure has an effect on the behavior of the sales team they are designed for. Every one. The tricky part is, many times those behaviors are the ones you don't want and didn't intend to create. Understanding the cause and effect of the plans you implement, and maintaining agility over necessary shifts in those plans, is the key to creating reward systems that support the results you want.

My favorite thinking on this topic is by Daniel Pink. His Ted Talk, "The Surprising Truth About What Motivates Us,"[6] is a great baseline for your thinking about how to design appropriate incentives for your team. Essentially, Pink explains how the degree of complexity of the task and the corresponding reward systems can either work together or against each other. For simple tasks, financial rewards associated with units of production are appropriate and effective. If you promise to pay me based on the number of shirts I press at the dry cleaner, or the number of aluminum soda cans I can collect in exchange for a few more recycling pennies, I will maximize my effort and my output. However, if you promise to pay me a sizable bonus for negotiating and completing contracts with the largest three new customers in our marketplace by the end of the quarter, provided those customers produce at least $250K in new business by the end of the fiscal year, it will be a different story. That's because the more complex a task is, the less effective straight financial incentives to complete them become. In fact, they may make the task less likely to be completed at all.

There's enough material about sales incentives for another book. Here, I'll share my philosophy about them based on my own experience and observations. For the purpose of this section, I'll treat commissions and bonus programs generically, and call them incentive plans.

Companies tend to make incentive plans very specific. Conventional wisdom says that the clearer they can be about the desired outcomes, the more likely the sales team will be able to understand and deliver those results. There's an underlying assumption that we salespeople are not that, well, smart. If you want a salesperson to produce, you need to be very specific about what you want, put a dollar value on it, and push the start button in the middle of his back.

I've seen two basic approaches by companies trying to motivate their salespeople. Consider two companies: Established Company and Emerging Company.

Established Company nurtures their existing customer relationships. They tweak their well-accepted products to refine performance. Stability and incremental growth satisfy their stakeholders. Employees are tenured and motivated by the values and integrity of Established Company.

Salespeople of Established Company are highly motivated, but their motivation isn't derived from their bonus plan. Their compensation includes an appropriate combination of salary and variable pay. Incentives are balanced across sales volume, customer retention, expense management and personal growth goals. The plan is predictable from year to year and reflects the priorities of the company. Employees think in terms of decades and plan to stay for a career.

Emerging Company is different. It is new to its marketplace. Emerging Company is focused on growth. Innovation and disruption are the priorities that color all decisions. New wins trump sustained customer relationships. Tenure is not a celebrated word at Emerging Company. New stars are hired to solve the growth dilemma of the day, hour, or moment. Lost customers and broken processes are glazed over by trumpeted successes. No time to stop and fix them. Just keep growing.

Employees at Emerging Company are individually motivated by upward mobility, maximizing bonus, surviving the frantic daily pace, or finding another place to work. Sales incentives at Emerging Company are fascinating. They change annually, or even more frequently. This year's incentive plan rewards the person who sells the shiny new product that is launching. It might also reward sales of the product that failed to sell well last year. If there is a sales shortfall during the current year, the incentive plan will change to chase that gap.

Salespeople at Emerging Company know that they have a continuously moving target. They don't act with a long range focus. They don't build enduring customer relationships. They are overly tactical and resort to gamesmanship to maximize their income. Eventually this comes back to bite Emerging Company. They have churned too many customers and employees. When they finally try to preserve their business by stabilizing their customer base, it doesn't work.

At Emerging Company, the salesperson of the year may be placed on a performance improvement plan the following year because he failed to pivot to the priority du jour. On the other hand, the salesperson of the year at Established Company tends to be the role model of the organization. The person whose portrait nobody would think twice about placing on the wall in the corporate corridors.

Use your influence to connect your sales incentive plan to your long range goals and objectives. Don't be tempted to narrow in on one single behavior and try to get more of that behavior by dangling a dollar in front of your team. Chances are you're not pressing shirts or collecting cans. Your business is more complicated than that. Your people are motivated more by doing a good job, getting honest real-time feedback, and feeling that they're helping a cause bigger than themselves. The money they earn should confirm the results they produce from those motivators. It doesn't cause them.

Plant directional flags in the distance

If you're a golfer you've seen them. That flag that sits in the middle of the fairway pointing you toward a hidden green. A blind shot. The flag is your only beacon directing your shot. You place all of your trust in the placement of that flag. Somebody has gone before you to survey the hole and guide your effort so you can reach the green safely. As a golfer, I really count on the placement of the directional flag.

Place these markers in all the right places so your team members can make all the right shots. The demands of the day pull your people right and pull them left. They get turned around trying to solve the problems that land in their lap. Your role as leader is to call out, "Over here!" Remind them of the waypoint they forgot about when the problem arrived and they became distracted. You still need them there. And they need to hear your clear voice to help them navigate in the direction of your intended destination.

In business, these markers take different forms. They could be the goals you agreed to when you sat down with your employee to construct their development plan at the start of the year. Perhaps it's that training you prescribed as part of his career plan. It might be a major project milestone or deadline, which needs to be held up high in order to rally a team that has descended into the weeds to solve the problem of today.

More than likely though, your flags will be of much higher order. When Green Mountain Coffee Roasters was about a $250 million company, our founder and CEO Bob Stiller shared his dream with us. He dreamed of a billion-dollar company. He said he could see it and we would get there. I was there and I shared the disbelief of everyone else who was present to hear Bob that day. I couldn't quite grasp Bob's dream; in fact I'm sure I chuckled under my breath. After all, I knew how hard it was to hit my team's current sales targets. A billion? Come on.

But, as time passed, we gradually moved in the direction of Bob's dream. Then we moved faster in that direction. Eventually we roared past that goal. And the next billion, and the next, and the next. It was astonishing to me that we had become what Bob had dreamed and visualized. You see, Bob held that flag up high so we could see it. And he kept holding it. It seemed like magic, but it really wasn't.

Our leader continuously reminded us where we were going. Even if we couldn't see it. Even though it seemed like a blind shot from where we stood. We trusted the flag he was holding up. He had seen the destination and knew where to aim.

Hold the directional flags up high for your team. They have so much to think about that is right in front of them. When they are able to briefly pick their heads up from all of those demands, help them spot the flags you are holding for them to see. They need to know you're still heading there. Once you build their confidence by bringing them safely to the destination a few times, they'll spot your flag sooner and travel faster. That's the magic.

Ask long view questions in short-term settings

You're an involved manager, not a seagull manager. You don't fly around above everyone and release your droppings all over the place.

Because you're an engaged manager, your people come to you with a range of questions and problems. They run the gamut from how to properly complete their expense report to how to handle a co-worker relationship to building their pitch to close a big deal. They count on your guidance for nearly everything they can't figure out on their own. In most cases the horizon for the issue they are trying to solve is close in. It's an immediate issue. Perhaps it's for a customer meeting that is days or weeks away. In less frequent cases it involves longer term thinking around business planning or their personal development.

Obviously, your focus should go beyond simply solving these problems for your team members. Develop their thinking into understanding that leads to the wisdom needed to solve the situations on their own. Bring a coaching style to each conversation so you are gradually preparing them to stand on their own feet, to acquire new perspective, and to make confident, strategic decisions. Teach them to fish rather than feeding them fish.

Essential to this coaching demeanor is getting into the habit of asking the big picture questions. Particularly when you are discussing business tactics, you must drive your team members to elevate their thinking. Get them thinking two and three steps ahead. What implications do today's decisions create for tomorrow's options and actions? One of the most difficult things for any of us to do is to take an outsider's view of the situation that surrounds us at the present moment. You must be the advocate for the outsider's vantage point in your coaching conversations with your team members. Draw them up and away from the crisis they are experiencing to allow them to look upon it with dispassionate eyes. Place them in a future state, looking back upon today's decision. Are they pleased with their choice? Did something unexpected occur as a result of their action? Help them gain the external perspective that tends to make the best choices more obvious, and develop that competency in them.

A word of caution. Remember, you must sustain your productive intent. You must foster efficient decision-making for yourself and your team. Sometimes you need to act before you have all the information you may need. Don't fall into the habit of taking every question up to 50,000 feet and going into a holding pattern there. You need to land. If your people think you won't get back on the ground they'll perceive you as being chronically theoretical. They'll stop coming to you with problems because you are wearing them out with abstract thinking. They'll start making answers up on their own behind a dark curtain, producing variably good and bad outcomes. You'll lose the pulse of your team and eventually fall out of touch with your business.

Help them think through problems. Give them additional higher order questions and implications to think about. Help them make choices if they need your help. Ideally though, just plant those seeds for them to consider and express your confidence in their ability to make the decision and run with it from that point. Support their actions and back them up. If things don't work out be there to help them sort it out. It's more important to have a confident team in positive forward motion than to get every decision exactly right.

Provide progress reports

You know about goals and their importance. You know about SMART goals.[7] Goals that are specific, measurable, achievable, results focused, and time bound. Goals are about being intentional about what you want and sustaining your energy and effort until they become reality.

Learning how to write goals is a practical skill you can acquire. There are countless resources to help you. Getting others aligned to the conscientious pursuit of achieving your goal is more difficult. But, with good goal development and adept communication and persuasion skills, you can become good at that part too. Delivering the results is another story.

The thousands of steps, missteps, and adjustments made between the declaration of your goal and the finish line are difficult. Much more difficult. How many times has your team stalled out on the way to achieving that big result? How often have you lost what you thought was the undying commitment of your team to make it to the finish line? It's probably happened to you just as it has to me. Why?

Setting that big hairy audacious goal is more than just an exercise in getting your team committed to doing specific work and delivering a particular result. It's a commitment you make to yourself and your team. A commitment of ownership to the goal and everything required to deliver the results you are calling for. You can't just break the huddle and tell your team to go get 'em. Unless you want to fail.

Leaders who launch a big initiative often brashly declare the results that will be achieved, then delegate the execution to their organization and step away. These are leaders whose teams and companies fail. I've seen leaders who delegate everything to their subordinates with a sink or swim management style. When the initiative is completed successfully, they proudly trumpet the results and even share some of the credit, although they don't know how it happened. On the other hand, when the project goes off the rails, they look for someone to blame and take the fall for them. In the worst cases, I've seen a blaming culture emerge in organizations, giving rise to a strong aversion for healthy risk-taking, resulting in stifled growth and minimal innovation.

If you're asking your team to achieve something that is over the moon, you must function as mission control. Be connected.

Spend time at every level of execution and every corner of the organization charged with completing the initiative. Talk to the people doing the work, not just the one-up managers who may have an incentive to put a positive spin on the progress to date. Hold broad meetings to deliver progress reports. Regularly reiterate the key steps of the initiatives, the need for execution of important approaching milestones, and the changes to the plan based on what you've learned since it started.

Ask everyone for feedback, and encourage dissent on any aspect of the initiative based on functional feasibility of the required work. Explore and investigate all feedback with the corresponding functional owner and put those insights back into the plan. Report back to the individual who asked the question or raised the objection, no matter where they sit on your organizational chart. Then report the findings and adjustments to the plan to the broader team in the form of a progress report. Repeat that process throughout the life of the project. Use your progress reports as the hard-wired connection between today's initiative and your long range focus.

There are lots of opportunities for you to delegate as an effective and efficient manager of others. This isn't one of them. When you set a transformational target for your organization, you own it. Your name is on it. Don't deflect that ownership by letting your team twist in the wind and hope somehow that you get the results you want. Take command. Hope is not a strategy.

LONG RANGE FOCUS: APPLY IT

My colleague James Jennings and I loved to use the NASA moon missions as a metaphor for the big things we wanted our team to achieve. We wanted them to reach high and believe in their ability to reach their destination. Normally the launches of such initiatives were perfect settings for the team to take an aspirational view of the mission we were placing them on. These initiatives were launched at planning summits or sales meetings in comfortable environments where everyone enjoyed the surroundings and when camaraderie was soaring. Getting folks to raise their hand and sign up for the challenge was the easy part.

It was the journey where we really tested our mettle as leaders. *Could we keep everyone as motivated and focused as we had on launch day? Would distractions of daily issues make that focus fade and cause some of the team to let others pick up the burden of completing the essential steps in the initiative?*

We knew the bumps would come and we would need to respond. When NASA goes to the moon, they don't just do some calculations up front, plug a straight line flight path into the computer, point the rocket on its way, then forget about things until it's time to land. They make adjustments all along the way. It's all those little adjustments that allowed the Apollo crews to reach the moon and return to earth.

James and I used to call this "managing the wobble." The spacecraft, or in our case the team, would wobble to and fro along the way to our goal. Our daily decisions, the outside environment, and other factors out of our control, would push and pull us off course from time to time. We knew that we had to pay attention to all these course deviations and get the team pointed back in the right direction.

As leader, you pull your team, your sponsors, and your customers in the direction of your goal. You run out a few steps ahead of everyone, then call them to join you. In order to be good at that, you need to understand the end game on a number of different fronts. Here are two areas you'll want to manage well so you can be standing where you want at the end of the journey, along with guidance to give to your constituents to minimize wobble.

Manage the customer relationship hierarchy

As we've discussed, each of your customers thinks about your company across a relationship hierarchy. You have customers that think of their relationship with your company as purely transactional. You also likely have customers that think of you as their trusted adviser. Somewhere in the middle you have relationships with customers who view you as a reliable supplier. More than transactional but less than trusted adviser. There is mutual trust and both parties are getting a balanced value from the relationship.

Your job is to drive decisions and actions within your company that move the customer relationship forward along that continuum. Not all customers will come to know you as their trusted adviser, but you should be pulling your organization in the direction of achieving that status. Your business risk is directly proportional to the number of your customers who view you as a transactional partner. For these customers, there are few barriers to switching suppliers. All your business with customers in this group is at risk.

The smallest of actions taken by people in your company add or subtract points with your customers:

> ➤ How did your company handle the latest product outage or damaged shipment?
> ➤ When the customer found himself in an unexpected pinch, did you expedite their order at no charge or let it go normally?

> ➤ When they were selling to a key client, did your salesperson show up or refuse to change his schedule?

There are hundreds of other small decisions that are made in a customer's life-cycle with your company. If each problem is held up against an objective of becoming the strategic adviser to all of our customers, answers are easy. You do what it takes to get you there. Influence all who make decisions affecting your customers, so that reaching that status remains paramount in everyone's minds. Pull your team and your organization in this direction.

Keep all your stakeholders connected and committed to your vision

You have a clear vision of where you want to take your business, your team, your division. You can see that destination and you articulate it regularly to your team. Make sure you're not operating in a bubble when it comes to making other important influencers aware of your long range goals.

Think about the big things you want to achieve. *Sales growth. Category leadership. New market entry.* You need allies. Your shoulders just aren't strong enough to carry everyone along on your success path. Your team has already bought in to your vision. You spend each day keeping them engaged and aligned with your vision. But who else is supporting you? Who else is touching your business in even the slightest way? Do they have any idea that you have such aspirational goals for your team and your organization?

Think about garnering support the way you would if you ran a political campaign. Turn your core principles into talking points. When you are having conversations with senior leaders, colleagues across functional departments, or with casual work acquaintances, share your vision in bite size pieces. Get reactions and tweak your messaging. But be consistent in how you talk about where you're taking your team and persistent in seeking input and support from others. Politicians repeat their main talking points over and over because their audience is always changing. If compelling enough, their ideas will take hold and their audience will help them spread the word. Your quest for support for your long range goals should be no different.

A leader I respect a great deal taught me an important lesson early on in my days of leading others. He told me that the way to get your ideas to take hold in an organization is not by directly advocating for them to senior leadership. It is not by cornering the CEO and laying a flawless sales pitch on her. The way to make your ideas stick is to give them away to others, so they can become their ideas. It's about building coalitions of people who adopt your vision because they hear your ideas from others in comfortable and non-confrontational ways. It's by creating this dynamic in multiple settings and varied occasions. Then when committees and leaders hear your same idea shared by third parties it rings a bell. Whether they associate the idea with you or not, that bell serves as a reminder and validation of an idea they've heard before. When this happens multiple times that validation turns to conviction that the idea has merit. When that idea connects back to you as the owner of its execution you'll have a new broad base of supporters that will make your heavy lifting feel much lighter.

Give your ideas stronger legs by building these coalitions and watch how others begin to support and accelerate the achievement of your critical long range goals.

Your role, as a leader in the center of your organization, is the most challenging role in your company. You sit at the intersection of today's deliverables and tomorrow's potential. You take the mission and vision of your company and turn it into sound strategy and tactics for your team. You take a theoretical possibility and transform it into a tangible action plan. No other role in your company demands this critical convergence of authority and accountability. Your company is disproportionately dependent on your ability to deliver results as you stand in that space.

Luckily, you are taking the long view in the decisions you make and the actions you take. Often longer than others around you. That leads to conflict. You must consider how you'll stand up to forces fighting your proper orientation to the long-term.

It's time to measure your managerial courage.

SIX

Managerial Courage

*"Adversity has the effect of eliciting talents which, in
prosperous circumstances, would have lain dormant."*

– Horace

Managerial Courage can take a variety of forms. Sometimes it is delivering bad news up the chain of command, information that is difficult but necessary to communicate to your boss. It might be letting an employee go, or even a group of employees if you are part of a reorganization that calls for that. It can also be a situation where you see an opportunity that nobody else sees, and only your persistence in convincing others will allow that opportunity to become a reality.

No matter the form and situation, managerial courage has several common elements. First, it is necessary. The information you share or the stand you take is absolutely essential for effective management of your business. Second, it is urgent. There is a time limit on the efficacy of the information or action you must take. Procrastinating will not make the issue go away, and will usually cause bigger problems. Third, it is an issue of your ownership. Nobody else can take on the challenge for you. You must step up, own it completely, and see it through. Finally, it affects other people. Failure to act, inform others, or otherwise address the issue with the appropriate people will adversely affect the lives of others. It's not about you or your anxieties related to stepping into the fray. Exercising managerial courage is an empathetic act. Failure to do so is a selfish act.

It's Not Just Math, It's About People

There are stories from my experience when I wish I had exercised more managerial courage. There are also stories that I could choose from where I displayed it. One story in particular stands out. My use of this competency ended up creating a successful outcome that no one saw as possible, including me.

In the fall of 2009 my company was involved in the acquisition of another coffee company. Tully's Coffee was a coffee roaster, wholesaler, and retail coffee shop operator in the Pacific Northwest. Tully's had its own interesting origin story, and a founder, Tom Tully O'Keefe, who built a company around a brand that embodied a fighting spirit to satisfy its consumers in the most competitive coffee marketplace on Earth. They operated like the little coffee company that could, battling their big competitor Starbucks in the coffee scene in Seattle and beyond. By 2009, however, financial reality had caught up to this $40 million company, and Green Mountain Coffee Roasters had agreed to purchase the company's wholesale businesses.

At the time, I led the West Zone of our Away from Home channel. My role was that of general manager in nature, managing 80 percent of the geography and 20 percent of the revenue for the division. It was green space for the company: untapped potential for new business. Though I wasn't part of the acquisition negotiations for the M & A team, I was brought in to help with the integration of the wholesale businesses. I had a distinct qualification from my fellow VP peers across our sales channels. I lived in Denver, so I was closest. About $10 million of the Tully's business would fold into my team's business, so it made sense that I'd be close to the implementation work. But I also took on the challenge as integration lead for the grocery and retail club stores. I was excited to be asked to run these parts of the acquisition, and for the experience I'd be able to pick up in the process.

My VP at the time told me to follow his lead. He had a playbook and an agenda. These things were straightforward: there were financial considerations driving decisions and when we came out on the other side we needed to be standing on financial ground at least as firm as we were when we went in. That meant all contracts had to be revised, renegotiated, or terminated. Customers had to be assigned to salespeople and outstanding issues needed to be inventoried and managed. Products needed to be consolidated over time to eliminate redundancy.

And then there were the people.

The culture of our company at the time was very appreciative. It centered on people as the key to our success. Our approach to the integration of the Tully's employees reflected that. Everyone from the Tully's team was offered a position with Green Mountain. In a company where employees had been living with the possibility of a Friday pink slip for some time, this was welcome news. Everyone was coming over and could rest assured that they would have a job.

Everyone except for the sales department, that is. After all, we already had salespeople. Surely we could absorb $10 million into the Away from Home business and assign the other $8 million or so in grocery and club stores into our existing sales teams. There were a total of ten people managing that business for Tully's. It turned into a math exercise for us. After all, salespeople are just a variable expense when you get down to it, right? My boss went into his playbook, consulted with Finance, and we determined that we would bring on one person, maybe two from the sales team. Ideally one.

That's what the math told us.

With our game plan in hand, we made our visit to Seattle for a day of due diligence with the Tully's sales leaders. We would meet the sales leaders and senior management team, take a tour of the operations, and get to know the Tully's business by reviewing customers, contracts, and people. After our day we would depart and proceed with our plan to keep the sales portion of the acquisition as lean as possible. Go in and get out. Nobody gets hurt. We arrived and exchanged pleasantries with the Tully's leaders and then headed for a conference room to start the work to cut out anything and anybody we didn't need.

To the outsider, the Tully's offices and operations were something less than state of the art. This company had built a wonderful reputation in the marketplace, a fabulous brand with real personality, and produced a delicious cup of coffee. They did it without the trappings of fancy offices or a slick manufacturing plant. The offices were old with lots of dark hallways and weary wood paneling. Workspaces were cramped. Floors creaked with each step. The coffee roasting plant was a multi-floor mash up of manufacturing process steps, which all happened in the former Rainier Beer brewery, a Seattle landmark. The building was iconic and the production flow was chaotic. Green coffee was received on one floor, then roasted on another, then packaged on another. Quality control and marketing were on yet another floor. In order for a coffee bean to travel all the way through the manufacturing process and end up on a truck headed out to a store, it had to ride on a freight elevator several times. Oh, and to load the trucks, Tully's had to shut down an adjacent busy road. Trucks literally stretched all the way across the road when it was time to unload raw materials or carry away finished product.

The overall picture was charming. And terrifying. *What exactly were we buying again? Was this bootstrapping company where so much of the operations still occurred on a hand-to-mouth basis now becoming part of our modern, more streamlined company?* OK, best not to worry about all that. That's someone else's problem. Time to get back to what I was brought in to focus on: which person from the sales organization did we need to bring on board? Back to the conference room.

I started meeting people. People who had been building this business, acquiring customers, and keeping them for life. Big customers: Boeing. University of Washington. Many others and all of them right under the nose of coffee giant Starbucks. When the stories started to surface about their customers, one thing was obvious. *Tully's customers loved Tully's people.* They loved the people that represented Tully's. People who showed up and solved problems. People who saved the day when customers ran out of coffee. People who chipped in and participated in special events. People who outworked their competitors day after day. When the giant tried to win these customers over by promising them favorable pricing or extra marketing support, they said no, thank you. They wouldn't switch. Not ever.

I left that day questioning the playbook. I continued conversations afterward with the contacts I had made. I kept learning about the sales team and the ways in which they solidified their customer relationships. It seemed to me that our mathematical equations didn't apply here. There was no equation in that playbook that could calculate the value of the Tully's salespeople showing up and working harder than anyone else in the marketplace. It became clear to me. I disagreed with the playbook. I had to make that known to the decision makers I was supporting and do it fast. I had to make my case to bring over the entire team. Everybody. It was my first involvement with an acquisition of any kind, but I needed to convince everyone of the potential risk I saw by using the old familiar approach we were about to apply.

I illustrated to our functional leaders that we faced great risks if we didn't bring the whole team over and sustain the business they had built. For Sales, I showed the risk of losing the big customers, who depended on a high touch relationship with their salesperson. Replacing large customers like these requires a long lead time, if we could even replace them at all. We'd be better off just keeping the Tully's sales team and keeping their customers happy. For Finance, I spoke along the same theme, and how the risk of losing even one of Tully's major accounts would affect the financial outcome of our acquisition. Our ability to acquire Tully's profitably would be impacted, and the subsequent reaction of the outside investment community would be negative. For Human Resources, I argued that terminating employees purely on the basis of a financial analysis was counter to our company's culture and values. We could not treat the sales group differently than other departments in good conscience. We owed it to them to bring them on board and support their transition to become productive in their new company.

In the end we brought everyone over to the new company as part of the integration. Over time, we became close and depended on each other. We added new customers and expanded relationships with those customers that were already loyal to Tully's and now became loyal to Green Mountain.

I found managerial courage I didn't know I had and used it to pursue an outcome I was completely committed to achieve. It was the only possible outcome I could accept based on what I saw, and how I felt. The payoff is that the relationships from the experience have endured. The people I met during the process worked on my teams for several years. We remain friends today. Management gained additional respect for my approach and my integrity.

The lessons I learned formed a foundation for approaching situations that would call for my courage. I think often about the impact my actions had on others, and I think just as much about what that impact would have been if I had not exercised managerial courage. It's this second part that keeps me motivated to step forward assertively when it is most difficult. Managerial courage requires you to care about others, and to advocate for outcomes that serve your compassionate purpose.

MANAGERIAL COURAGE: RECOGNIZE IT

What Exactly Is Managerial Courage and When Will I Need It?

So what then is managerial courage? What does it look like when it is present, and when it is absent? How will you know when to exercise it and when to save it for later?

I view managerial courage as a resource similar to political capital. You earn it over time, and you can't spend what you don't have.

In *For Your Improvement*,[8] by Michael M. Lombardo and Robert W. Eichinger, managerial courage is characterized by describing observable behaviors. The skill is evident when a person:

> ➤ Doesn't hold back critical information
> ➤ Lets others know exactly where they stand and provides meaningful and complete feedback to them
> ➤ Faces up to problems with people, whether they manage them or report to them, promptly and directly
> ➤ Is not afraid to take a difficult or unpopular action when necessary, and they do it without wasting precious time

This is a competency that requires balance and judgment. I've seen few leaders who are skilled at deploying it all of the time. Like many skills, we tend to draw upon this one only when we have the optimal energy and focus on the situation before us. More commonly, I've seen this skill overused or avoided by managers I've known. Each of us has a tendency to do one or the other.

Overdoing it

I've seen the leader who overdoes it when it comes to giving their manager bad news about what's going on in the marketplace. Distributors are angry about the latest price increase from the manufacturer. They're threatening to switch to another supplier. *We can expect to lose 20 percent of the business and then we'll be in even worse shape than before we decided to raise prices.* Reaction: We need to bring a trade incentive to our top distributors so they'll stay with us. It's the only way to keep them on board.

Senior management buys the assessment. After all, the front-line manager is closer to the action and knows the distributors better than they do. Management capitulates and together they devise a growth program for the distributor. But there's another wrinkle. The distributor is not satisfied with getting paid an incentive later for their business. After all, they helped you build this business. They'll need an advance on their incentive plan so they can maintain the pricing they extend to their end users. That's the only way they can keep their base end user customers and work with them to grow the business. Besides, you can't expand business with a customer who isn't buying from you, right?

So our leader goes back to senior management and tells them that their distributor was pleased with the growth program, but needs the advance on the payments or they'll have to go with another supplier. Senior leadership is back where they started. They are not intimate enough with the distributor to sort through the real situation and there's no time to do that. They accept their manager's pitch once again and begin to pay up front for the incentive.

After a few more back and forth negotiation points, supplier and distributor settle on the economic and reporting parameters of the growth incentive. Time passes, and the business has not grown. In fact it is now declining slightly. There was no real effort to expand the business in the marketplace. Once the storm passed, the sales leader, salespeople, and the distributor went back to business as usual. The manufacturer and the distributor now dispute the data that says there was no justification for the incentive payout. The manufacturer has an awful choice: they can let it go, or try to recover funds from their distributor via surcharge. They avoid the obvious conflict, and they let it go. The economics of their price increase have been undermined. Rather than gaining, they have lost revenue and the relationship with their distributor is damaged.

And the sales leader who believed she bravely brought the urgent information to her senior leadership has gone to the well once too often. Her credibility is questioned. The next time she needs management support on a critical situation she'll instead garner their scrutiny.

Avoiding it

There is another leader. This leader does not deploy managerial courage when he needs to. He avoids conflict, sometimes at all costs. Whether it is upward or downward in the organization, he defers tough actions until they are past the point of positive influence. One example is in the way he deals with problem employees.

One member of the team isn't pulling his weight. He takes shortcuts with customers. He makes his numbers through side deals and cuts corners with free products and unauthorized incentives. He encourages his customers to poach business from the company's customers in other channels by going outside the defined parameters of products and pricing. In meetings, he is clearly separate from the team. His ideas are independent and his contributions are self-centered. He looks at his phone while others are presenting. He is obviously affecting team morale. The rest of the team wishes he wasn't there at all.

The leader, however, looks the other way. After all, the salesperson's numbers look great and he's hitting all of his targets. As long as that's happening, the situation can't be that bad. That's what it's all about anyway, right? But the team is now losing confidence with their leader. They dread his meetings and don't buy into the directives he gives them. Sometimes he even holds up his narcissistic salesperson as the example everyone should emulate. He lauds his attainment of sales targets and prods others to follow his example. The final straw happens when he receives the Salesperson of the Year award at the company's sales meeting. The camel's back is now broken. The leader has lost his sales team, now in full mutiny. His shielding and avoidance of reality brands him as a person who should not be in management, and his leadership arc in his company has peaked for good.

Leaders who are adept at exercising managerial courage understand balance. They understand discretion. Compassionate leaders like these are empathetic with the people all around them and appreciate the effects of their actions or non-actions. Managerial courage calls for the leader to defer to no definitive master, but rather to meet others where they are. Such leaders embrace an appreciation that shared responsibility is necessary to make transparent decisions with full and accurate information.

Here are three scenarios where managerial courage will come in handy for you as leader, spanning your internal relationships and your ability to spot new opportunities from your unique vantage point.

Managing up

As a front-line salesperson, you kept your boss informed. Things are a little different now that you are in her shoes. What is new is that you have to use the insights you gain from your team, your own observations, and your sound judgment to keep a wider upstream audience informed about your business. It goes beyond keeping your one-up manager informed about good news, bad news, and dilemmas that need their assistance to solve. Scope has grown dramatically for you.

Let's start with your manager. You want a relationship that is multi-dimensional. Strive to be a dependable lieutenant. You need to keep your leader informed, but that doesn't mean you constantly drop problems in her lap.

It's important to have regular conversations with your leader, and let her know where you stand on each issue in terms of competence and confidence. When an issue is brand new to you, you need guidance and encouragement. When you're more of an expert on an issue, you'll want to take the approach of informing your leader about the problem, how you've assessed the situation and available options, and the course of action you've decided to take. In between these extremes is a continuum of your competence and confidence, depending on the specific situation. Develop a relationship with your leader about where you stand on that continuum, setting the expectation that you'll be up front about it, and conduct conversations with her where you can obtain the coaching approach you need. These are the keys to effectively tackling any challenge together.

Beyond your direct supervisor, a number of stakeholders also need to hear from you, either directly or through your manager, about business issues affecting their area of functional responsibility. You now need to be more anticipatory in the way you synthesize signals from your team members, customers, and competitors. You have to play scenarios out several steps ahead to understand what might happen next. What are the implications for Finance, Operations, and Human Resources? What types of questions will those departments have for you or your manager based on the action you take?

Elevate your vision of the landscape so you can begin to build a holistic picture of your business. You are in the catbird seat. Your view of the field of play is better than anyone else's. Leverage that advantage by making continuous assessments and informing other leaders who cannot see what you see. They will come to count on you if you exercise this advantage. If you defer to others, or otherwise fail to place the appropriate value on your position, you'll earn the perception that you are myopic and self-interested. You don't seek out progressive disruption. You share information only to your own pleasure and interest. You will slip from your standing and instead be seen as a broken record when it comes to delivering recurring problems surrounding the business.

Terminating employees

I'd like to say this is a tough one for every manager, but I can't. I've seen enough managers who don't have a problem with firing people. For our purposes, however, let's agree that this is one of the most difficult tasks one person has to do to another person. If it's not hard for you to do, then frankly, I don't want to hang out with you.

There are two main scenarios in which it becomes necessary to terminate an employee: for cause and as part of an organizational change.

When terminating an employee for cause, one of two circumstances will occur. First, an employee has violated the rules. They've done something unethical, illegal, or otherwise prohibited by your company's code of conduct. Second, they have failed to achieve acceptable performance levels. You've agreed on clear goals and they have not been attained. You've cleared out any extenuating factors and arrived on a common understanding that the performance is less than required for the position.

Let's agree on a few assumptions. You are a thorough manager. If there is a violation of policy, you and your company have made the rules clearly available to the employee and communicated them regularly so there's no surprise. It's a black and white issue and the reason for termination is obvious to all. Likewise, if there is a performance problem, you've also been clear about communicating goals and progress against them all along. You've offered support, assistance, and training to encourage the employee to succeed. You've followed your company's policy around performance improvement plans and now you're at the point of termination. Nobody, including the employee, should be surprised.

For termination that occurs as a result of an organizational change or financial hardship, you'll want to be careful. You certainly want to have a partner in your company's Human Resource and Legal functions to ensure you are taking the proper steps and are protected from scrutiny about how you handle the termination. If you are the decision-maker about who stays and who goes, make sure you are making decisions equitably. There are unique challenges when you are working with a team of decision makers on a reorganization that results in significant change in roles or elimination of jobs.

During organizational change, it is critical to defer talking about specific people until the end of the process. First agree on the business problems you're trying to solve, the structure you need to attack them, and the roles, not people, you'll need to carry out your plan. In other words, align first on the specific functional requirements for the business before you talk about people by name. If you are part of the reorganization team, you must insist that the team avoids talking about actual people until the end. Stop conversations that head down this path and defer them until later. I've seen teams do this part well and build team structures with a valid and strong foundation. I've seen other teams talk about people too early in the process and end up looking like they were choosing players for a pickup game in gym class. Talk about ugly.

Now that we're comfortable that you're following protocols for your company and making business decisions rather than playing favorites, let's talk about the emotional side of letting someone go. For a long time for me, this was the hardest part of being in management. There were times when I faced the reality of the need to let an employee go, and wished I could wave a magic wand, avoid that responsibility, and get back to work. I had a hard time looking another person in the eyes, and telling them I was taking their job away from them. I had so much sympathy for that person. Why did my company need me to do this, anyway?

Appreciating the difference between sympathy and empathy helped me in these situations. Yes, I had sympathy for the person I was letting go. I felt sorry for them, for their situation. That was as true with the first person I had to terminate as it was with the last one. The key to gaining a balance in my emotions in this area came when I began to think of other people.

I thought about the other people on the employee's team. Those who were picking up the slack on the team's deliverables. Those who were working harder to fill the gaps. I thought about employees across my company who counted on me to run my department effectively so their efforts could have a positive impact on our business. I thought about customers who were being underserved by their salesperson, and who deserved better. I thought about shareholders who trusted me to deliver maximum value in return for their investment in my company. I had empathy for all these people. I stood in their shoes and imagined what they were feeling. Their expectations of me.

When I focused on this entire picture, it became easier for me to take the difficult steps to terminate my employee. There are a few things I tried to do every time I had to have one of these meetings. They were always face to face. That sounds obvious but I've known plenty of managers who fired employees over the phone. My conversations have been direct but the time I allowed for the meeting was always generous, even open ended. I don't do Fridays. Nobody needs such an event like this leaving them feeling steamrollered over a weekend. I allowed space for emotion. Sometimes there were tears, anger, and confusion. Sometimes hugs and sometimes not. I tried to understand the experience from the employee's perspective and I didn't block out parts just because they made me uncomfortable.

Don't be a robot when you have to terminate someone. That's a person across the table. Exercise your managerial courage, be compassionate, and take your time. Leave him as whole as you can so he can take a positive next step in his life.

Courageously pursuing the unseen opportunity

The "what if" questions are scenarios nobody is thinking deeply about, but they keep you up at night. As a visionary leader, your wheels must always be turning. You are constantly reading the horizon and spotting opportunities that need to be explored, pursued, and captured. And while others may bring you their top of mind ideas about what you should be doing to expand your business, few are giving those ideas the depth of thought required to really decide whether they are attractive enough to shift focus and go after them. That's your job.

Something you should start doing right away is to begin writing a situation analysis of your business. You need a long-form narrative that portrays the current conditions of your business:

> What is the market environment?
> Who are your competitors and what are their advantages and vulnerabilities?
> Who are your customers and your desired customers?
> How penetrated are you in the businesses where your customers compete?
> How far do your products go toward satisfying the needs of the marketplace?
> Do you have an organization that is properly resourced and aligned against the demands of the marketplace?

You need a rigorous analysis of the strengths, weaknesses, opportunities, and threats (SWOT) and a gap analysis across all the dimensions of your business.

For each business unit I led over my career, it was important to me to author this document and keep it alive. I needed the story of my business. There is no substitute for taking the time to create the long-form narrative of your business and keeping it updated every time you learn something new. Whether that takes the form of a business plan or situation analysis or some other document, you need to be the sole authority on what is happening and what is possible for the business you are leading. There are no short cuts. You can't wing it.

Your advantage is that you can bounce every new idea and potential game changing opportunity against your living analysis. Ideas that are potential winners will easily find their place in a gap or problem you've identified. Ideas that come out of left field and should return there will be obvious as well.

Distribute your situation analysis to your team, your one-up manager, senior leaders who have an eye on you and your business, and functional leaders with whom you work across your company. I've always favored printing a hard copy and handing these out, especially to my team. I realize it is hard on the trees, especially since it is updated regularly. I've found though that unless this is something people can throw into their briefcase and pull out on an airplane, it will go unread. Look for ways to save trees in other areas and make this a physical representation of your business that everyone can digest. Make it real.

When it is time to raise a new opportunity and gain support for the initiative few people are thinking about, your narrative will serve as the backbone of your pitch. Your managerial courage will be fortified by your thorough understanding of your business reality. Ideas that are raised that don't have this foundation will land like random brainstorming and will be forgotten shortly after the meeting in which they are raised. Ideas that fit into your plan will quickly garner genuine support and your constituents will rapidly move from why questions onto how questions. You'll have credibility as the authoritative critical thinker on your business.

One final note. Being a visionary sometimes means saying no to a proposition around which others are coalescing. After all, nobody knows your business as deeply as you do because nobody else has thought about it as thoroughly as you have. In addition to finding the gold in unseen opportunities, you also must deliver today's results. An idea that takes you and your team's eyes off the ball of pursuing what you're accountable for today is not a good idea, unless that idea comes with new resources and a guarantee that it won't harm current work.

Write the story of your business and revise it every day to be the leader who sees the unseen opportunity and avoids chasing each shiny object that appears before you. That takes managerial courage enabled by the confidence of knowing your business better than anyone else.

MANAGERIAL COURAGE: APPLY IT

Managerial courage leaves a trail of observable evidence. The circles of people who believe they can count on you expand. Your opinion is sought out in times of extreme crisis or opportunity. Others know you don't operate in clichés, outdated rules of thumb, or expired playbooks. You meet every challenge with an open mind as a thought leader in your organization.

But be on guard for behaviors that can undermine your managerial courage. Exercise astute self-awareness to recognize these behaviors in your leadership style.

Be cautious about overplaying your strengths and tendencies

The manager who cries wolf too often and seeks organizational intervention to solve her team's problems creates an atmosphere of pessimism. That behavior will permeate the team and result in a whining culture, not a winning one. If you direct too much energy toward internal negotiations on budgets and bonuses, you'll build a perception that you are more *of* your team than *above* your team. Senior management will grow weary of the predictable interactions with you, and begin to doubt that you can lead effectively. Managerial courage demands your discretion. Like political capital, you must build your account balances and spend wisely. When you call for support for your positions, you want others to be fully engaged and aligned with your thinking and guidance. They won't go there if you are constantly driving them onto your point of view on recurring problems.

Don't be afraid of the truth

Be the thought leader and truth advocate in your organization. Even when information is difficult, recognize that it is merely data that will inform your next action or next decision. It is natural to want to avoid bad news, or let it pass through your personal filter to soften it by only examining the elements that you think you can manage. Develop a mindset that you'll be more empowered by having all the available information. The decisions you make with the full view of the situation will always be better than those made downstream of a filter of self-deception. Create an environment where others can bring you any type of news without fear of your reaction or your ill treatment of the messenger.

You are not a soothsayer

You cannot see the future. Be careful not to fall into the trap of convincing others that you can. I've seen leaders with a book of experience shorten due diligence and debate by portraying their ability to see the future based on their past experience. The war stories they invoke are meant to convince others that they know the way forward. They use it as an offensive tactic to stifle analysis and ensure that they get to make all the decisions. Their path may or may not lead to success over the problem at hand, but they maintain power by unilaterally making the calls on people and tactics. When results fall short they shine a light on the shortcomings of individuals or improper execution of tactics as they see them from their command position. You can be sure that this leader will not be personally harmed when it comes time to figure out what went wrong. He has already moved on to getting out in front of the next crisis and calling the shots again. This is not managerial courage... and it won't serve you in the long run.

Play it straight. Take an honest and assertive approach to tackling your responsibilities and building your reputation as the steady leader that others can follow. Managerial courage doesn't mean you lead every charge up the hill. But it does call for you to be available and accountable. Always. Keep that in mind as you think about how to deploy this skill.

Your portfolio of hard skills is now robust. While there is always more to learn, your core is solid. You are a strategic thinker with a well-rounded assortment of functional assets. You've got an orientation toward producing results and you apply sound judgment to the challenges you embrace. You think about the future and the impact today's decisions have on your long range goals. You apply all of your developing strengths with the managerial courage of a sustaining leader.

It's time to shift your focus from how you view the world, to how the world views you. Time to round out your repertoire of hard skills with some softer ones. Time to become the modern compassionate leader.

Let's begin with empathy. As you'll see, this has already shown up in many of the hard skills already described.

PART II

The Soft Skills

SEVEN

Empathy

"I fashion the expression of my face, as accurately as possible, in accordance with the expression of his, and then wait to see what thoughts or sentiments arise in my mind or heart, as if to match or correspond with the expression."
— *Edgar Allan Poe*

When I went to business school in the 1980s and in my early years working for companies, I heard a strong message: there is no space for emotion in business. Leave your emotional baggage at the door. Walk and talk in an objective manner. Never use the word *feel*. Always use the word *think*. If you've got problems in your life, leave them at home. Don't bring them to the office. You'll have plenty of time to wallow in those things when you go home at the end of the day.

That never sat well with me. Of course I wanted to take an objective and thoughtful approach to the business situations I encountered. Clear thinking is the key to finding solutions, no doubt about that. But I walked through my early career years with a detachment from others that was counter to my upbringing. It wasn't who I was as a person. It certainly wasn't how I behaved with my family or friends. I had become two people. A relaxed and affable person outside of work, and a reserved technician at the office and with customers. I knew that was consistent with my training in business school and the guidance I received from the leaders I was exposed to, but it didn't feel right to me.

It wasn't until I had the opportunity to begin leading others that the lights slowly began to come up. I no longer had only a passing interest in how people around me were doing, how they were feeling. I now had a vested interest in making sure they felt supported, appreciated, confident, and capable of achieving great things. True, it served my own purpose to make sure my people were moving confidently through each day with a smile and a swagger. But beyond that, I realized that I did actually care about them, as people. I wanted to get close to them. To understand them. To get to know them and their families. *What were they interested in and when they wanted to have fun, what did they do? What were they struggling with on a personal level? What hopes and dreams did they have for themselves and for people that mattered to them?*

Business school didn't teach me this stuff. A few of my early managers exercised great empathetic leadership, but most did not. We punched out of our emotional time clock when we came to work and punched back in when we went home. When I became responsible for the performance of others that was no longer good enough for me.

An Unexpected Wake-Up Call

My most vivid lesson about empathy came during my very first sales role at Mack Trucks. I was twenty-four years old. I had just completed Mack's nine month sales training program and had been selling used trucks for a few months at the company's Philadelphia branch. I wasn't breaking any sales records yet, but I was selling enough to earn decent commissions and my confidence was building. I was young and single, so having a little cash in my pocket felt pretty satisfying.

I was working the floor on a weekday, which meant I was first in the queue for any walk-in customers. At this point in my career I wasn't the best prospector, and cold-calling wasn't my favorite activity. Working the floor meant that I had a decent chance of meeting a customer who was ready to buy a truck. All I had to do was be friendly, and try to match him up with something we had in inventory or a truck I could pull from another Mack branch. If I could do these simple things I could make a sale and pocket commissions.

One of my early morning activities was to print an inventory report and then walk the yard to check out any new trucks that had come in. On this particular Wednesday there were two late-model Macks that had just come into inventory the prior afternoon. They were very clean and had low miles. They were traded at a good number, which is to say that the trade-in value wasn't improperly inflated in order to close the sale of the new trucks that customer bought. Since I made 25 percent of the profit on the used trucks I sold, I was in for a good commission if I could sell one or both of them.

The trucks were nearly identical. They had a glossy maroon finish with no scratches and both had a sleeper cab. There was one difference. One truck had a single rear axle and the other had a dual rear axle. The dual axle was much more common for our trucks, and made the truck capable of hauling maximum cargo up to a gross vehicle weight of 80,000 pounds. The single axle truck was only rated up to 46,000 pounds. While the overall capacity was less on the single axle tractor, it was desirable for lower-weight niche applications, such as to haul cargo that required a large cubic capacity trailer but didn't weigh as much.

Late that morning a man entered the branch. His name was John Evans. He seemed to be in his mid-forties. John owned and operated a small used car dealership in Marlton, New Jersey, a short drive over the Delaware River from our branch in northeast Philadelphia. He would travel to auctions, buy two or three cars he thought he could sell, then haul them back to his dealership. He'd fix them up a bit and then put them out on his lot to sell. He was currently paying someone else to bring the trucks back to Marlton, and he wanted to do that part himself to be more profitable.

Small dealers like John usually have a car carrier truck commonly referred to as a hot shot. It's a single rear axle tractor with a sleeper cab that can tow a small car hauler trailer. Because cars take up more space than they weigh, these operators don't need a full 80,000-pound capacity in their rigs. Since they are often small operations, the sleeper cab is essential. They can travel farther distances to auctions and not waste money on hotel rooms. The hot shot truck is fairly rare, and finding a used one in good shape is rarer still. John's description of his situation made my sales bell ring. I had the perfect vehicle. It was exactly what he wanted from a functional standpoint and it was in his price range. We completed a successful test drive and began negotiating.

There were two scenarios I encountered when it came to negotiations with customers at Mack. The first was when their offer was underwater. In other words, they offered to buy a truck for a price that was less than the inventory value plus my commission. The second scenario was when the offer came in above the inventory value plus commission, or in the money. In both cases, I would tell the customer I had to get my manager's approval. But when a deal was in the black, it was my call on how much to negotiate.

At 25 percent commission on any profit, I knew that for every hundred dollars I could negotiate I would pocket twenty-five dollars in commissions. So when I went back to the office on these deals, I would usually chat with the staff, or see if there were any donuts left, or do something else to kill a little time. Then I'd come back and tell the customer what my new lowest acceptable price was and go from there.

On this day, my manager wasn't even in the building. He was out visiting a customer. The truck we were negotiating was in the money. So I did my normal routine, disappeared for a few minutes, and came back with a counter offer. I was pretty excited about the potential sale though, so I decided I wouldn't be overly greedy. We landed on a price that worked for both of us and signed the papers.

Now one other thing I would do with my manager during a negotiation would be to check one last time that the truck was still available. For trucks that had been at the branch for a while, this was important. Inventory reports weren't updated every day, so occasionally a truck would be sold but still show up as available in inventory. Since my boss wasn't there that day, I skipped that step on this deal. But I wasn't worried, since the truck had only come in the night before. There really wasn't any chance it had been sold, I thought.

I made arrangements with John that we would get the truck prepped for him to pick it up Saturday. That meant we would change all the fluids and filters and detail the vehicle. I also needed to send it out to the body company to have a new fifth wheel installed. That's the round plate on top of the back rails of the tractor that the trailer connects into. All that work would be done by Saturday morning for John to take delivery.

I was excited. I calculated my commission. I knew I'd be able to cover my bills that month and have a little spending money to boot. When I saw my manager the next morning I went straight up to him to tell him about my deal. His response stopped me dead in my tracks. "You can't sell that truck. That truck is sold." My jaw dropped. He told me that one of the other salespeople had a verbal deal on the truck the same day and my deal wasn't a deal. I protested unsuccessfully. I asked him what I was supposed to do, since I had already taken a deposit and scheduled prep work and delivery.

My boss told me to tell the customer that there was something wrong with the truck and we had to send it back to the person who traded it in. He offered to sell him the matching truck with the dual rear axle to the customer at the same price. More truck, same price. That should work, right?

It didn't feel right to me, but I really needed the sale. I called John Evans and explained it the way my boss told me to. He was disappointed and reluctant to accept the other truck. But finally he agreed. I assured him we'd still have everything ready for Saturday, and he agreed to take delivery then.

Saturday morning came. It was a bright sunny spring morning. John arrived at the branch, and he didn't look happy. We greeted, and I told him that his truck was still at the body company but it was ready. The body company was nearby so he offered to drive us there in his car, and I would drive the truck back to the branch where we would finalize his paperwork.

To this day it remains the most memorable car ride of my life.

Shortly after we started out on the twenty-minute drive, John began to speak. "There was nothing wrong with that truck," he said. "You guys sold that truck to somebody else. I know you did." My mouth went dry and my face turned red. At this point I didn't know if he actually knew that fact or if he was making a loose accusation. It didn't matter. He was right and I wasn't going to try to defend myself. I was speechless. John then spent the rest of the ride lecturing me, as an elder would lecture a young person, about the importance of honesty in life. About the importance of fair play. About treating people the way you would want to be treated. Basic stuff. Things I had learned as a kid. This lesson, though, hit me hard.

I felt terrible. By the time we reached the body company, I was in tears. I was sobbing. John had reached deep inside me and woken up a part of me that I had suppressed in the hopes of being successful, of making sales, of earning commissions. But it was the way he did it that left a permanent mark on me as a person. He spoke to me from a place of caring. He understood who I was and where I was standing. He saw that I was a young man in need of guidance which needed to come from a place of empathy. He was angry at his situation, but he set that aside to step inside my world, and speak to me in a compassionate tone about who I was and what I needed to think about to become the person I was meant to be.

I pulled myself together and we finished our business at the body company. John drove his car back to the Mack branch and I drove the truck, deeply reflecting all the way back about what he had said to me. We finished the transaction, shook hands, and John left to go back to Marlton. But I was changed. I had just received a dramatic wake up call. It would change my understanding of what empathy means, especially in a business relationship.

A week later, I drove to John's business to deliver the final paperwork from our deal. When I greeted John, he was up to his elbows in grease. He was doing repairs to cars he had purchased and was preparing for sale. I appreciated that this man was putting his whole self into his business. I saw pictures of his family and understood who he was working to support. He told me how a few things had broken on the truck I sold him and that he had fixed them. I thanked him again for buying the truck from me and for talking with me the way he had. We shook hands again and I headed back to Philly.

I never spoke to John Evans after that day. I saw his truck on the road once or twice hauling a few used cars, and he was surely driving. But my experience has remained vivid since those two weeks in 1988. It was the first time I experienced a customer as a whole person, and not just as a partial person who was there to serve my needs. I had to be available and vulnerable to do that. I was available, because I was in John's car. And, I was vulnerable, because I allowed him to open up a part of me that desperately needed a light shined upon it.

Our customers, employees, colleagues, and managers are full persons. To deny or ignore that and focus only on how they are useful to us, is to miss out on the deeper rewards of a life lived with true empathy as its foundation. I learned my biggest lesson about empathy because John Evans turned the tables on me. He made the effort to understand me. To step inside my situation. To become me for a moment. He was the customer and I was the salesperson, but our roles didn't matter. It was a person to person connection.

That's where empathy lives.

EMPATHY: RECOGNIZE IT

You'll Know It When You See It, and When You Don't

My vivid learning experience about the value of an empathetic perspective occurred by accident. Empathy hadn't been on my radar at all. As I reflect some thirty years later, it is ironic that I learned my most enduring lesson about empathy by receiving it, rather than practicing it. It is clear that John Evans lived an empathetic life, he wasn't just doing situational empathy.

Most of us think of *empathy* as an emotion similar to *sympathy*. If sympathy is our tendency to feel sorry for another person, or have pity for them based on their situation, then empathy is simply a muted degree of that same emotion. You understand the situation of the other person, but you stop at the doorstep of feeling pity for them. Sympathy connotes an inherent sense of superiority. You know you're better off than that poor chap, and you're grateful not to be in his shoes. For many of us, empathy isn't really much different. You just stop yourself from acknowledging your full feelings about that person.

In business, we strive for empathy and avoid sympathy. We train ourselves to limit our emotional investment in customers and employees. After all, you may find yourself in an uncomfortable situation when it's time for hard negotiations with your customer, or when it's time to discipline or terminate an employee. If you keep things professional, you'll be able to handle those situations with cold objectivity. How inspirational.

The fact is, that with only the hard skills we've discussed to this point in the book, you can go far. Many do. But you can't go all the way to compassionate leadership unless you master the critical soft skills, and empathy is that doorway.

Empathy is much more than understanding, or appreciating another person's feelings. To reach a deeper understanding, you have to pursue empathy at an intensely emotional level, not just intellectually. You have to do even more than walking in the person's shoes, so to speak. You have to *become* that person. You must use your full imagination to place yourself in their life and to see the horizon as they see it with their eyes. This is a journey of immersion, not simply a fact-finding mission. You cannot approach it as a technician.

Empathy is not a skill you pull out of the drawer when you need it, and put back when you're through with it. It's not something you do *to* people. It's not a trick or a tactic. Empathy is a foundational mindset about the way you relate to other people. It becomes who you *are*, not how you *act*.

Empathy requires that you pay attention to surroundings and circumstances, always. Empathetic people ask curious questions because they want to know what is at the core of the people and situations they encounter. Their curiosity is not self-serving. It is generous and open-minded. It allows that the answers to the questions they ask may lead them to the unknown and uncomfortable. They don't fear those dimensions but see them as a necessary path toward deep understanding of others in their pursuit of mutually beneficial outcomes. Outcomes where each person's emotional realities are respected and honored. Where honest revelation conquers false choice and self-deception.

Developing an empathetic mindset tends to happen over time rather than suddenly. It must be practiced. In my case, a single experience served as the wakeup call. It became the catalyst for me to begin asking the singular question that empathetic people ask. *Why? Why did that person behave in that way? Why did the customer say no to my offer? Why isn't my team behind me on this important initiative?* As a compassionate leader, ask the why question constantly to get at the core drivers of the outcomes you are creating.

Your capacity to lead with empathy shows up when you are striving to hit a sales objective, navigating crises, seeking support from colleagues, or deciding how much to delegate. Below are four examples of situations where empathy and lack of empathy can create different results for you as a leader.

You need your team's support to deliver a sales objective

Setting sales goals and delivering the results is more art than science, no matter how those goals are set. I've worked in organizations where goals were built from the bottom up and also from the top down. Neither approach is inherently more valid than the other in my view. In either environment, getting your team aligned behind the goals and working in sync to deliver the results is your objective as leader. I've seen leaders succeed and fail in that endeavor in direct proportion to their ability to lead with empathy.

Let's consider an example of when goals are set by senior management and delivered to your team. From your seat, there is little ambiguity about the goals. Your leaders have handed them to you and you are accountable to make them reality. You have two behavioral choices when it comes to implementation.

<u>Behavior 1 - Low Empathy</u>. You can turn to your team, explain that management has given us these goals, and we have to deliver the results. There is no negotiation and no debate. You have done the math and allocated the sales targets across your team. You inform them of their deliverables and after a brief meeting, you send everyone on their way to

figure out how they'll attack the goal and deliver results. This is an exercise in delegation for you. You give your team the challenge and tell them to go get it done.

Consequence/outcome: Your team leaves the meeting at worst disgusted, and at best confused. Individuals are on their own. Even though you told them to come to you if they need help, they don't have the confidence in you to provide that help. They don't come to you. They also don't collaborate with each other on how to achieve the goals. Even if a little cooperative brainstorming happens, it doesn't result in meaningful leverage against the overall target. You haven't exactly established a culture of teamwork. You've created an environment of survival of the fittest. Those who deliver results are rewarded and those who don't are punished or managed out of the company. In the end, the combined performance of your team members does not result in achieving your sales goals. And you now have a much bigger problem. Your team is fundamentally damaged.

<u>Behavior 2 - High Empathy</u>. In this option, your goals are also set by senior management. This time, however, you spend time with your superiors to understand them fully before turning to your team. You ask questions.

> ➤ How do your goals contribute to the success of the organization?
> ➤ How do they relate to the goals of other divisions and how is your team's contribution prioritized by the organization compared to other work across the company?
> ➤ If your goals have significant stretch, what incremental resources are available and how and when will those be provided?

> ➢ What is the consistent messaging that will be used throughout the organization to assure all contributors that the goals are essential but also achievable?
> ➢ What critical support can you count on from sponsors and functional leaders across your organization?

After you explore these and other critical questions with your senior management, you turn to your team. You start by understanding where they sit. They are about to receive their sales target for the year. They are thinking about their kids' college tuition, their mortgage payment, their retirement plan. Everything you talk about will be translated into that context in their minds. You must approach your delivery with that sensitivity.

You explain the critical business dynamics behind the goals. You talk about what is happening in the marketplace and why the objectives you are laying out are valid and essential for the division and the company. You project that you are bought in to the goals, because you are. You've done the due diligence and challenged areas where you had questions. You believe the goals are valid and achievable. You insist on questions from your team about anything with which they are uncomfortable. You address the questions and agree to follow up on any that remain open. You allow plenty of time to talk everything through.

Finally, you do something else different than in the first behavior choice. You commit to your team that you are in it with them, and you ask for their help. You are all in it together. If a few people achieve their goals but the team does not, then the team loses. Even though individuals might do OK financially, the team is more important. You tell them that they can't leave the room unless the team is committed to achieving the goal as a unit. Anything standing in the way of that mindset must be surfaced and addressed.

You outline a method of working toward the goals in project management style. You define key roles needed to execute the work and draw volunteers to take on those roles from the team. You agree on communication protocols. Most importantly, you stress to your team that you are fully committed to supporting their work. You make yourself available for problem-solving, customer meetings, and any additional discussion needed for everyone to internalize the goals. You become and remain completely present for your team.

Consequence/outcome: Your team leaves this meeting feeling supported and empowered. They know you've thoroughly vetted the goals assigned to you, and you haven't agreed to anything that is out of reach or unrealistic. They know they have the access they need to you and by proxy, to senior management. They trust that you carry their voice throughout the organization. Each individual team member knows that her peers are just as committed as she is to achieving the desired results. She knows that because of the project plan you outlined, there will be no late surprises coming from other team members that will undermine the plan too late in the game. There is a strong sense that the team is more important than any one person. Each person understands he must carry his weight. You asked for each person's help. There is shared obligation across the team.

Takeaway: Teams like those in Behavior 2 develop a tradition of winning. When a short term challenge comes their way, they are not fazed by it. They simply take a deep breath, go into their learned mode of working that you have infused, and tackle it together. Individual stress is lower on these teams, because there is less mystery about what they need to accomplish. Communication is better. Morale is stronger. They do not stall out. People on the team want to stay on the team. People on other teams want to join this one. I've seen it.

The obvious differences in the two behaviors are stark. Chances are you've used or seen blended combinations of the two in your own planning cycles. Even when your goals are built from the bottom-up, or perhaps in some other hybrid fashion, you face the same dynamics with your team. Sales objectives built from the team level still have to ascend through your management structure for approval. In almost all cases they will be challenged, by you as well as senior management. You can count on additional stretch getting bolted onto the plan. You'll face the same challenge of getting your team aligned and committed to that goal. Approaching your goal setting and plan implementation with empathy will make a big difference in the near term success of your team against its goals and on your legacy as a compassionate leader who consistently delivers results.

Your team member has a personal crisis

The longer you serve in a leadership role, the more likely you'll be faced with a personal situation that challenges your character as a compassionate leader. Today's companies are not configured to support the leader very well when these situations arise. True, there are employee policies in place in most companies that extend the required family or medical leave, maternity leave, and other accommodations to help the employee in a difficult time. While it is certainly better that we have these provisions than it was for workers in the past, these benefits provide only a modest financial safety net to the employee in crisis and are designed in a one size fits all manner. Life situations that draw your employees' focus away from work create emotional stress. Their attention is drawn to a crisis they haven't planned for, and there is new worry that their job may be affected.

You will encounter all kinds of scenarios that require your empathy, that require you to get close to your team members and understand them as a complete person, not just as the owner of a set of tasks. Some of them are obvious and affect your employee directly. Pregnancies, cancer, divorce, and other interruptions to routine life occur all the time. The larger your team, the more likely you'll experience these directly with your team members. Additionally, we are all members of families and illness and loss are a part of each of our family lives. Often we only know about these hardships if we have close personal relationships with these people. It's easy to identify with their struggles and to be an empathetic friend. For those with whom we are not close, their burdens are shouldered in the shadows, and our line of sight is limited.

One thing is clear, however. The crisis that affects your team member is intensely personal for him. His emotions dominate his thoughts in every activity and across every obligation he has as an adult person. Despite the best coping mechanisms or his ability to shield others from his trauma, by definition he becomes a different person. As a leader you can't ignore this dynamic. You have to step into his life. Even if you have been an empathetic leader to this point, you have to go further.

In my role as leader I've experienced many life-changing situations through my team members and colleagues. Big ones. A team member who battled and beat breast cancer. Others with pregnancies. Employees who suffered losses in their families. A child of a team member who suffered a permanent disability in a car accident. The sudden death of a dear colleague. Many more.

While company policies for employees in personal crises may sometimes be adequate, often they are not. You have to commit to picking up the slack. While you can't do that financially, there are other things you can do:

> Rally your team members to cover some of the work. Step in yourself to stay connected to important customers.

> Relieve your employee from special projects so she can focus on the essential stuff. Find the work-related stress points in her life and relieve them.

> Most importantly, let your employee know that her job is not at risk. If she is a rising star, assure her that not only will her job be held for her if she has to take extended time off, but her status as a valued employee will be preserved as well. She will not take a step backward.

> Speak to the rest of the team and be clear with them that they can expect the same treatment if they are ever in a crisis.

This is the type of leadership that will go unseen outside of your team. Others in your organization won't notice how you have supported your team member. They may not even be aware of the crisis she is facing. Your team member will remember. And so will your team. Your bonds within your team will strengthen immeasurably. The culture that emanates from these situations will define the way your team operates and you'll grow as a result. No challenge will overwhelm you once you demonstrate how you can get your people through the really big things.

You need the support of other department heads

Success doesn't occur in a vacuum. If it were only left up to individual performance, it would be easy. All you would need is your own personal initiative, determination, and follow through. It would be like a golf swing. You perfect your swing and make the score you are shooting for.

Business is more like an orchestra. All musicians must produce sound from their instrument at the right tone, volume, and timing to create beautiful music. When a single musician is misaligned with that process the result is undesirable, even disturbing. It takes more than a great conductor to keep everyone playing the same tune properly, it takes the cooperation and common motivation of each musician in the orchestra, regardless if they would rather be playing a different tune or launching into a solo performance. The conductor is part leader and part therapist. He spends time getting to know each of the musicians and crafts his instructions into their language, so his priorities can become theirs.

The fact is, your goals start out in conflict with every other department in your company because the likelihood all of your goals were written together and well synchronized is nearly zero. Your sales goals are not yours alone. They involve marketing, production, fulfillment, service, finance, accounting, and any other functional areas that touch you and your customers. The leaders in these departments, your functional counterparts, all have their own priorities. Your sales goals, whether built from the ground or delivered to you from on high, did not fully consider the priorities of these departments when they were built. Likewise, Accounting didn't check to see if their goal to reduce outstanding receivables conflicted with your sales growth initiatives. Neither did Fulfillment when they decided to reduce days-on-hand inventory. Neither did Service when they elected to outsource service calls to a third-party vendor.

So why are sales leaders so shocked when their fellow functional leaders don't drop everything when they are called on to support the new great Sales initiative? I've seen it over and over again. Sales leaders get their teams all fired up to pursue the latest sales strategy and then they hit a major internal roadblock from a department that didn't get the memo. Conflict ensues and the problem is escalated to senior management to decide whose priority to override. The organization wastes precious time figuring out why the goals were not better aligned. Everyone's goals get watered down a bit. There are hard feelings between the sales leader and the other functional leads. A quarter of the year is lost. The sales team is disillusioned because you started them down the wrong road. The team will not hit the aspirational results you had in mind for the year, and your leadership veneer has a few new scratches.

So much planning wasted. What happened?

The missing element in this typical scene is empathy. As leader, you have a responsibility to insert yourself into the planning process with your functional colleagues. If your organization doesn't routinely facilitate that coordination, then go to each of the functional leaders yourself and insist that you participate in their planning process. Invite each one of them into yours. At a minimum, spend time with each leader for a mutual briefing on your goals and how you plan to reach them. Surface points of intersection and of course, conflict. Seek out opportunities to support each other's goals and even accelerate achievement, by developing synergistic new ideas.

Then turn to your team. Ideally, have the functional leaders each articulate their priorities to your team. Alternatively, brief your team on the priorities of these departments based on your own understanding. Build your action plans with a basis in the reality of capabilities across your organization, given your newly-developed broad perspective. Keep your fellow functional leads apprised of your team's progress and seek out the same updates from their departments.

Don't fall into the trap that many sales leaders face, adopting a victim mindset when their initiatives fall on the ground because another department doesn't share the same urgency. More than likely, that sales leader never made a sincere effort to get to know his fellow functional leaders. He never developed a constructive relationship or personal rapport. He never spent the time to understand the other leader's goals and the rationale behind them. He practiced the self-deception many leaders practice, falsely believing that everyone else appreciated how important his priorities were. He proceeded behind the illusion that his goals were implicitly paramount to the organization, and that all other stakeholders would accept and support them.

Be the leader that enthusiastically embraces the ambiguity inherent in today's complex organizations. The leader known for actively engaging with your fellow leader counterparts. Understand what they're up against in being successful, and invite them into your world to see your challenges. There is no substitute for warm personal contact when you're trying to make beautiful music together. Don't pretend that you can do it all yourself, or by overpowering your colleagues with political maneuvers.

When empathy is missing...the delegation myth

Perhaps the most common example of the empathy gap in to-day's organizations has to do with delegating. According to the philosophy that has taken hold in American businesses over the past thirty years on the way to create the most effective management development systems, great managers are created by giving them responsibility, holding them account-able, and letting the cream rise to the top. The best manag-ers are power delegators. They don't get caught in the weeds. They stay above the fray. They assign tasks, set deadlines, and distribute rewards and consequences.

This myth is self-fulfilling for the hyper-delegating leader. The less he knows about the operational realities of the business, the more his priorities will become detached from the performance of the company's core functions. This widening gap undermines strategy and ultimately creates organizations that can't keep pace with the leader's vision.

It's true that as leader you can't live deep in the details. You have too much on your plate to be intimately involved in everything your team is doing. But you can't use that as an excuse to be a helicopter or seagull manager. You must be engaged enough so you can step in without needing a crash course on a situation every time someone raises their hand for help. You also have to keep your head above the crowd so you can see the broader horizon when your guidance is needed. I've reported to managers that walked beside me on my success journey. I've also reported to managers that I needed to give a 101 refresher course on my business every time I had a question for them.

The management development approach of move up or move out that has dominated companies over the last thirty years is, in my opinion, in sharp conflict with a compassionate leadership approach rooted in genuine empathy. While it has certainly produced thousands of competent managers in hundreds of companies, it has undoubtedly discarded many high-potential managers by not nurturing their development in a deadline-intensive environment. It has done so at a cost to people and companies that has manifested itself in the culture gap widely evident in these organizations today.

You can be an effective delegator and an empathetic leader. These are not mutually exclusive. Find your balance by ensuring you have the pulse of your team. Understand their opportunities and challenges. Understand what's keeping them up at night. Dig for details to help your understanding of a situation. When you understand, stop digging and take appropriate action.

EMPATHY: APPLY IT

My most important advice to you is to slow down. Go slower. Leading with empathy is in fundamental conflict with today's multi-tasking life. You can't build a scorecard for it. You can't easily put it into your measurable employee development plan. They won't be handing out the Empathetic Leader of the Year Award at this year's national sales conference.

Empathy tests decisiveness. Since your days in business school and through your management training you were trained to be decisive. Ambiguity is your enemy as an effective leader. Knock it down when you see it and make decisions. Keep yourself and your team moving. That's what great managers do.

I encourage you to think differently. Whether you are su-premely confident or you are facing confounding ambiguities, empathy is a muscle you must exercise. Here are two good habits you can develop to get you in shape and keep you fit.

Guard against overconfidence

As leader, you already have broader visibility than your team. When issues arise, chances are good that you'll have the most fully informed perspective and you're likely to be capable of making a good decision on your own, most of the time. My experience has been, when I feel 100 percent confident about making a decision, that's when I need to bring others in. I've learned that in those situations, I am the expert about what I already know, but I also don't know what I don't know. I sometimes convince myself there is no more available relevant information. And I'm consistently wrong about that.

The overconfident leader is also usually the low empathy leader, because he is not vulnerable enough to acknowledge that there is always more to learn. Leaders need to keep their teams engaged on a wide variety of decision-making processes. From small decisions to big ones, greater perspective almost always results in better outcomes. Facilitate fluid dialogue with those around you so you are routinely discussing issues and broadening your understanding of factors and choices available to you. You can't do that unless you have a genuine appreciation for other points of view, and for the people contributing those.

If you catch yourself feeling overconfident, make your decisions more slowly.

Embrace the open space

When you engage an employee, a team, or another functional area in your company, think of it as if you're walking into a garden. Take time. Walk around and experience everything rather than just looking for that one thing you came to see or take. Stay in one spot for a while and allow things in that garden to show up in your time of pause. Take it all in. The air. The smells. The sounds. The vibe. Understand that in that garden are people who, like you, are living a life. They are seeing everything with their own eyes, through the unique filters of their lives. Everything that happens around them is relevant mainly in the way it affects them personally.

I had the experience in my career to work for a company that rapidly traveled through all the growth phases in a relatively short period of time. As we traversed from our early growth phase to high and hyper growth phases into maturity, I saw a number of tenured employees begin to leave the company. Some left voluntarily and some transitioned out of the company because of restructuring. I was a twenty-year employee, and many of these departures affected me personally. I hated to see friends leave the company. These were people with whom I had shared a journey, building a small coffee company into a formidable consumer products power. I thought about how it made me feel to see them go. I thought about what it meant for my tenure. *How long would I be here? What would our company become with so much change happening?*

I thought about me. I thought about what it meant for me. I barely thought about what each person who was departing might be going through.

When I decided to leave the company myself, I got to see this dynamic from the other side of the equation. When it came time to tell my team of thirty-five people that I was leaving, I was floored. People were very emotional. My personal conversations confirmed that there was mutual sadness that we wouldn't have regular contact anymore. But it was their first reactions that caught my attention.

It was clear to me that each person's initial response was to think about what this meant to them. *Who will my new boss be? Should I apply for Jim's job? What will this mean to the current strategy, the current projects I'm working on? What does all this mean to* me?

Pay attention to this. Everyone reacts to new events they encounter through their filters about what it means to them personally. We are all wired this way. If you don't allow yourself the time and space to walk around in other people's gardens, you'll be surprised by their behavior and their reaction to your behavior every time. If you do spend that time and soak it all in, you'll walk comfortably as a leader who is at ease with any interaction, based on your empathetic understanding of those around you.

But empathy is not a one-way mirror. It isn't something you *do to* someone.

Invite others into your garden. In Chapter One I shared the example of how I kicked things off with a new team I was launching. I skipped the PowerPoint presentation and spoke from the heart. I shared my personal mission statement. I asked for everyone's commitment to do their best and support each other each day. I assured them that when we hit a crisis, we would get through it together, and when we had a win, we would celebrate together. While other leaders were starting off by articulating their key performance indicators and other scoreboard metrics, I wanted to get to the heart of the matter. I wanted to get to their hearts.

The best way for you to establish a culture of empathy in your organization is to let people into your heart. Let them see what you're all about. Share everything you can about your business philosophy, your personal life outside of work, the ways you like to have fun, to learn, and your struggles. Steer clear of motivations to do this with ego, or to generate envy or sympathy. Just be real. You are a person just like everyone else. When leaders rise up through organizations, there is a tendency to think of them as superhuman. They become less fallible. They become less approachable. They become less engaged.

Don't be that leader. The very best I've been around are the same person at the summit as they were in base camp. The responsibilities change as you move up the organization chart, but you'll need the same competencies, interpersonal skills, and values that got you there. Start today while you are rising in your company. Get real and stay real with your team and the people around you. The more approachable and genuine your leadership style is, the more others will let you in. You'll learn more about them and about the situations that confront you. Your successes will accumulate, your team will feel fulfilled, and your star will continue rising.

Can your people see you through the glass? If they can't, what you think is empathy will feel more like sympathy to others. That won't get you to compassionate leadership.

But empathy alone won't get you there either. You need to complement your empathy with transparency.

EIGHT

Transparency

> *"To conceal anything from those to whom I am attached,*
> *is not in my nature. I can never close my lips where*
> *I have opened my heart."*
> — *Charles Dickens*

Transparency, like empathy, must be part of your wiring and not merely a tactic you use occasionally. It must be who you are and not just what you do. Since it is impossible to spot the myriad of situations when transparency is essential, you must commit to continuous and seamless transparency in your management style. No light switch here. Will you be an opaque or transparent leader? Do you believe power flows from the principle of abundance or scarcity?

Many scenarios provide you the opportunity to display one or the other. Perhaps none are more wide-ranging in their impact than organizational change.

The Dark Curtain of Organizational Change

Reorganization. Restructuring. Realignment. Organizational rationalization.

These euphemisms veil tumultuous change occurring in organizations everywhere. Affecting real people. The translation of each of these terms is that lives are about to be turned upside down. Get ready for a ride on your very own emotional roller coaster.

I had a number of encounters with major organizational change in my career, sometimes as passenger, sometimes as crew member, and sometimes as conductor. I saw decisions made with the best of intentions that resulted in personal hardships and lasting scars. I saw leaders who normally operated in a transparent style hang a black curtain between themselves and the teams they were shuffling. They did this in the spirit of reducing anxiety and preserving confidentiality. The result was often the opposite of their intended effect. Unfortunately, lessons learned during these cycles were and are quickly forgotten as the organization gets back to business as usual and mistakes are repeated during the next reorganization initiative.

Passenger

Philadelphia. My first experience with a major shakeup happened after only my second year in sales working for Mack Trucks. I was pretty much a happy-go-lucky young salesperson, living hand to mouth by selling trucks and counting commissions. I tried to make dollars from my good months stretch across my lean months, and have fun on my weekends. Life was stressful financially, but it was simple and enjoyable from the standpoint that my responsibilities were limited and manageable. I was single and relatively carefree. Life was pretty good.

On one June Friday afternoon, my colleague Brett and I decided to wrap the week a little early and go grab a beer. It was around three o'clock, and nobody wanted to hear from a sales rep then anyway. We knew we weren't selling any more trucks that week. No sooner did we sit down at the bar than our pagers both went off. Yes, our pagers. If you're too young to remember those, the drill was simple. We wore them on our belt. When they beeped or vibrated, they flashed a phone number on the tiny screen. You took down the number, found the nearest pay phone, and called to see what the emergency was. It was the high technology of the day.

We both looked at our pagers. It was the number of the branch. Often this meant that a customer had walked in and asked for me. It meant that I might sell a truck, or it might also mean that a truck that I had sold had broken down and the customer wanted me to take care of it. It was usually a coin flip over whether it was good or bad news.

However, Brett and I both received our page to call the branch at the same time. That could mean only one thing. The boss wanted us for something. It couldn't be good. We both called in to the receptionist. One of us could have called to find out what was up, but we didn't want to reveal that we were together at the bar. We were pretty shrewd that way.

The message was brief. Our boss wanted everyone back to the office immediately for a meeting and it couldn't be discussed over the phone. We hustled back to the branch and went into the boss's office. The news was brief and direct. We were closing in sixty days. Everyone would be out of a job. Mack had decided to close all the company-owned stores and sell their trucks through their independent dealer network only.

I was stunned. This was quite an announcement to hit people with on a Friday afternoon. People who worked at the branch for many years were devastated. The sight and sound of ladies crying in the office affected me in a way I hadn't anticipated. I couldn't believe the suddenness of the announcement. And on a Friday? It seemed insensitive to send people home for the weekend with such awful news. Once it set in for me, though, I wasn't that fazed. I was young and single. My obligations were modest. Once I burned through my meager severance package, I could collect unemployment and still be OK for a while as I looked for a new job. Selling trucks was pretty tough anyway, and wherever I landed would be at least a little easier, right?

We staggered through the next sixty days, eventually said goodbye to each other and headed in our different directions. The experience left me curious. How could a company who depended on the hard work from such a good group of employees make a decision like this in such an impersonal way? Could I expect this type of situation to come up again and again in my career? Was there any way to see this coming and to prepare myself better than I had?

I was merely a passenger on this ride and I was unwittingly committed to go wherever the driver wanted to take me. I didn't like that.

Crew member

Vermont. Fifteen years later I had a different seat on the reorganization train. I was a leader of a national sales team. Our newly hired Senior Vice President held a vision to shift from our current organization by channel of business into a geographic-based team with sales responsibility across all channels. It was logical. We had salespeople living in the same city but only talking to half of our customers there. This would give us leverage and efficiency in the way we deployed our sales assets.

This time I became a member of the reorganization team. Even though I was one of the people who would be significantly impacted, I earned a seat at the leadership table of the implementation team. I had input to the process. My insights about people, their talents, and their limitations were incorporated into the decisions we made. But my input had limits. I was allowed to contribute to the details about where we placed people and about how we defined their roles. But I was not asked for input on the process itself. Our boss already had his playbook on that. The playbook was not up for discussion.

At the time, this was actually a comfort to me. It was comforting that somebody else had an end to end process we could follow to make changes to our organization and to people's lives. I was relieved that it wouldn't all fall on my shoulders. I could tell people that we had to do things in a certain way, because that's how you do these things. They couldn't blame me, since I hadn't come up with all this.

Besides, I had my own situation to think about. My role was changing. I was offered a choice VP position in the new structure, but it was on the other side of the country. If I wanted to stay aboard I would have to move from Philadelphia to Denver. I agreed to take on a whole new team, new business responsibilities, and new customers. In fact, I was embarking on developing an untapped market for the company, so I had an opportunity to build something from the ground up with my new team. If my leader could take the process part off my mind and my plate, that was fine. I checked my healthy skepticism at the door of the project to keep my stress level at a manageable level. I even squelched my own anxieties about uprooting my family.

According to the playbook, confidentiality was essential. Giving anyone the slightest clue about what we were working on would create anxiety and unnecessary water cooler chatter on the team. If they got distracted worrying about what was coming they'd become immobilized. We'd lose our sales focus and miss our numbers. There was zero tolerance for leaks. When it was determined that a member of the core team shared some inside information with a person in the sales organization, he was cut from the planning process. This was just how you did it.

When it was time for implementation, we went into tactical formation. We followed a rigid cadence. One-to-one, face to face meetings were scheduled with each level of the new management structure. Personnel were asked to fly to a city for a meeting at a hotel with no explanation. Role assignments were handed out, and managers were asked to accept their role on the spot or exit the company. There was no negotiation or individual advocacy for a different job.

As we worked our way down through the management tiers of the organization, we eventually reached the broader team. Here again, everyone was asked to fly to a city for a meeting of unknown purpose. As people began to gather in airports, shuttles, and the hotel, the new faces they saw made it clear that they were now on a new team. Ultimately everyone settled into a large meeting room for the full download on what was happening. They had a new job, a new title, a new boss, and new customers. The priorities were flashed on a screen while everyone's heads were spinning with changes. They learned that their business cards would be delivered in six weeks, but that it was time to get to work. They had two options. Embrace the new assignment or leave the company.

Everyone boarded planes, flew back home, then started burning up the phone lines talking with each other about what had just happened to them. It was shock and awe for all. It would take weeks and in some cases months before individuals regained their momentum and fully embraced the changes. Some never did and eventually left the company.

I trusted the process. It felt like we were making correct decisions, but our people were bruised. It turned out to be more than a technical exercise; something was missing.

Conductor

Boston. Six years later. I had been through a handful of reorganizations and had seen them from different vantage points. Now it was my turn as a principal player. My turn to make the big decisions about process, implementation, and strategy. I was part of a leadership team, but I had wider autonomy about how to proceed. It was time to bring everything I had learned into the current process.

Though I got a lot right, I didn't get everything right. I brought influence to the team and redirected thinking when I could. Even in situations where I couldn't shift the course of the team, I was able to guide my own thinking and take the steps that were consistent with my acquired wisdom about these projects. If you show me the way enough times, I'm bound to catch on sooner or later.

The business reasons for reorganizing were again rational. We were consolidating two redundant sales organizations; a little more than a hundred people were affected. This time we were moving from a geographic organizational structure back to one defined by channels of business. I had come to accept that there was no single correct structure for companies, just the one that makes sense in the current business situation.

We were moving from six Vice Presidents down to four, and fortunately I was among the four.

While we agreed on confidentiality about the reorganization, information began to reach the team. It's inevitable. When you notice your manager is always going to meetings all of a sudden, and isn't talking about them, something big is obviously happening. Some leaders were keeping it quiet, others were overtly talking to their teams about the changes that were coming. There was jockeying for position among managers and salespeople in the organization. Politicking was rampant.

For my part, I tried to keep it all aboveboard. I didn't go out of my way to inform my team of the inner workings of the planning team. But when engaged, I didn't hesitate to share my vision for the food service business and that I was embarked on a project to make that vision a reality. I kept it professional and stopped any role lobbying when I encountered it. If you weren't willing to advance my thinking about my vision, then it was hard for me to think about how you fit into that picture. But, if you wanted to talk about strategy, then I was all in with you. My thinking continued to develop during these conversations. I learned that managers don't have to do everything behind a black curtain, even if there are some things you don't bring out into the light until the end of the process. I began to appreciate the value of transparency in forming the new team.

In the end, the new team that I assembled gathered for our kickoff meeting. It was the meeting I spoke of earlier, when I ditched my fancy slides and simply talked with them about where we were going. They wanted in. Nobody asked for a different job. Nobody asked to renegotiate. People spoke of how they thought they could help, what they offered in terms of experience, and invited everyone to tap into them for knowledge.

This team launched a journey that resulted in many wins. We added millions of dollars in new business. We began a team relationship that I cherish to this day. There was more than just respect across the team. There was love. We were bonded together in the mutual acceptance we had of our mission and the commitment of everyone on the team to that mission. I'm convinced that the positive dynamic of that team was born by a more compassionate approach to the reorganization work. I respected the playbook and accepted protocols, but I remembered that we were changing the lives of real people. Rather than shielding them from information to protect their feelings, I treated them as grownups. I painted the picture of where we were going and invited them to be a part of that picture with me. We walked together with a shared purpose.

Three different scenarios. Three different roles. So what did I learn?

Understanding how to behave transparently in a reorganization is a lot like buying a house, or riding a bike. You must go through it a few times to really learn how to do it. But it isn't rocket science, and there isn't a secret playbook. It's about understanding that you are affecting the lives of people. People who care about the same things in their lives as you do in yours. Security. Prosperity. Safety. Opportunity. Approach your reorganization responsibilities as a leader with transparency and compassion. Begin with a clear vision of where you want to stand in the future and bring others with you.

Secrecy and mystery should not be your primary tools if you are leading significant organizational change. They may get you to the finish line with less drama, but in a reorganization, that finish line is only your new starting line. Remain open with your people and they won't come to a dead stop when it's really time to get going.

TRANSPARENCY: RECOGNIZE IT

Power and the Abundance or Scarcity Mindset

Reorganizations aren't the only occasions in which companies face a dilemma about transparency. And while it's always been curious to me why leaders hang the black curtain during major change initiatives while trying to keep the light of day shining at other times, this chapter isn't about reorganization protocol. It's about a management philosophy rooted in trust that shows up in the form of leaders who open up to their teams and the people around them. Transparency in action.

Transparency is a power equation. It's about your core belief about where power should be seated and how that power can generate the greatest leverage for business success. There are basically two schools of thought about the role of transparent leadership and its ability to generate power.

All leaders in business hold essentially the same priorities. They want their team to succeed and achieve its goals. They want the financial rewards that accompany that success. They want to progress in their careers and to keep their personal momentum in their organization. But there are two divergent mindsets on how to pursue those aspirations.

The opaque leader: scarcity mindset

Opaque Leader is outwardly confident. She has built her reputation in the company first by being an accomplished individual contributor. She consistently delivered above her sales plan and even pioneered much of the business success the company now enjoys. She did it the hard way. She wrote the book on selling the company's products before the book existed. New salespeople come to her to hear about how she built the business in the early days. When a strategic dilemma surfaces, people turn to her for insights on how a similar situation was solved in the past. When it comes to the sales game, her credibility is unchallenged in the company.

But now she leads a bigger team. Success is no longer determined by her own individual ingenuity, but by the success she can generate through her team. That's leverage. And while she has assembled a competent team, her scarcity mindset keeps her from going all the way in bestowing her confidence upon them. It keeps her from leading with transparency. After all, she wrote the book in this company. Her team will always be a few notches below in terms of the insights they can bring to bear to solve any given problem, right?

Opaque Leader manages her team on a *need to know* basis. She is a distributor of information, but there is a catch. The information that flows to her team is first digested, synthesized, and then translated for distribution to the team. She doesn't have tolerance for loose ends, or for sharing information that is not yet fully baked. After all, her capital in the company is built upon the foundation of knowing. To release information that contains open questions, issues that she is not yet ready to answer with a position that preempts challenge, would subtract from her reputation as perpetual expert.

When it comes to managing sales activities, she keeps her team on a short leash. She is uncomfortable with freelancing when it comes to their selling tactics. As a result, her team is less nimble than they could be. When an unforeseen challenge arises, salespeople reach back to her for a solution. They are less apt to think on their feet. Over time, they'll stop bringing new challenges to her because the delays they experience result in lost sales. Customers see them as unresponsive to their needs. The salespeople may begin making up solutions on the spot and keeping those from their leader, or they may lose interest in the difficult sales altogether. Growth will slow, morale will dim, and the team will eventually break down.

Opaque Leader includes only a very tight circle of people in her planning cycles, and she holds most of the cards. Plans are built in the dark. It's not exactly a mad scientist approach, but very few people ever get to enter the laboratory, and there are no windows to look through. The team spends the planning cycle on pins and needles. They know a plan is being cooked up, but they don't know whether they will stay the current course or embark on an entirely new direction. As the launch date approaches, some salespeople do everything they can to squeeze sales into the current year, while others become stalled out in a worry about what is coming next.

When the plan is delivered, it takes the team days or weeks to digest the new directives. They start behind schedule because their leader's scarcity mindset held back information that would have helped them prepare for a fast start. Unless the sales pipeline was full and fertile going into the new year, the first month's sales target is lost and the second is in serious jeopardy. The team does its best to finish the first quarter respectably and then works double time to make up the shortfall during the year. Midway through the fourth quarter, the cycle begins again.

There are a few telltale characteristics of this team. Vertical communication from the field is quite varied. Astute salespeople spend inordinate amounts of time lobbying their leader toward their views. Salespeople who have become weary of the one-way communication flow and the lack of transparent leadership pull back. The leader doesn't hear about what they are seeing in the marketplace, critical customer trends, or competitive threats. The squeaky wheels begin to dominate the leader's thinking, and the team's inertia moves in that direction, for better or worse.

Another characteristic is the amount of water cooler talk that builds within this team. All of that information and energy has to go somewhere. Since the leader has placed a virtual cap on vertical communication and dissemination of information in general, the water cooler is the relief valve. Eventually the banter leaks from the team and into other corners of the company. The leader's reputation is infected, and her future as a leader in the company may fall into jeopardy. Her team is likewise vulnerable. They may be branded as the team of whiners unless a senior leader can see through the noise and properly diagnose the problems.

The tenure of Opaque Leader can be alarmingly brief. The team that starts out following loyally because of the leader's incoming reputation will sour on her quickly. Frustration and disappointment set in. There may even be scarred feelings from being shut down publicly when individuals drive for more transparency. It is nearly inevitable that the leader will fizzle out within a few years unless a significant intervention and rehabilitation occurs. Those outside fixes are rare, and rarely successful for Opaque Leader.

The transparent leader: abundance mindset

Transparent Leader is different. He has also been a success in the organization, first as an individual contributor on the sales team and later as a leader of sales teams. His teams have consistently delivered the results he was accountable for. He leads with a quiet confidence, and it is more likely that you'll hear about the successes of his team from others than you will from him. He is a low ego leader. His teams follow his example. They win without dancing in the end zone. His team is likely to be seen helping each other out, making the diving catch when needed, and looking for opportunities to help the whole team succeed. What is different about this leader?

First, he trusts his people to handle information that is full of ambiguity. He treats them as professionals. As adults. He understands that having partial information is more important than having no information. Rather than keep his team in the dark on evolving issues, he opens the curtain so they can see the sausage-making in action. He recognizes that the keys to the unanswered questions probably lie with his team that lives closer to the customers. Even when he can't identify the person who is best suited to help on a current problem, his abundance mindset tells him that by opening up the problem to everyone, a path toward the best answer will emerge.

His team knows that they are in stride with their leader, not a few calculated steps behind. They feel like partners in the business, crafting strategy jointly and contributing to decision making in real time. Anxiety related to future plans and strategy shifts are not a factor. That's because this leader solicits input on strategy formulation, on competitive threats, on day-to-day challenges. Members of this team know that they may be asked at any time for their point of view on a mission critical topic, so they stay more fully engaged. They feel valued because their input is not only asked for, it's an important part of the business process. It is an implicit part of their membership on this team. Employees want to join this team, and once they're there, they want to stay.

Transparent Leader has high self-awareness and avoids self-deception. He knows that just because he has ascended to the manager's chair, he doesn't have a monopoly on knowledge and insight. He lays down principles about how the team will work together, not rules about how members must behave. His abundance mindset attracts intense loyalty, which he feels in return for the members of his team. He hires well. Since he is not under a false burden of having to be the smartest person in the room, he knows that filling the room with people better than he will lead to greater success. He takes pride in building a team of highly engaged and competent employees, and he champions team members who are promoted to greater roles in the company.

When awards and recognition begin to come, Transparent Leader deflects the praise and holds up his employees. When the occasional fecal fan collision happens, he stands up and takes responsibility. His team leaps to his aid and vows to correct the situation as a show of commitment to their trusted leader.

Planning cycles are more open. There is no lag between the time of the finished plan and the subsequent required action from his team, because he kept them informed and involved, and they are already up to speed. He is more likely to deliver the results he commits to in the first month, the first quarter, and the entire year. There is no shock and awe, just trust and transparency. His leadership is sustainable and his teams stay together longer and deliver multiple years of successful results.

Why do these two types of leaders exist in organizations today? After all, a scarcity mindset, by definition, is in conflict with the virtue of transparency. My observations tell me it comes down to the way people derive power from information.

Opaque Leader tends to derive power from holding information. If she holds information that you do not yet have, she has leverage and ultimately power over you. By dosing out that information to you, she can maintain her edge over you. Opaque Leader always has the *scoop*. She sees information as a commodity, and if she can keep a higher inventory of that commodity than you, she'll keep her advantage over you.

This leader operates with a scarcity mindset. There is only so much information, resources, people, political capital, etc. to be possessed. She is solely focused on maximizing her share of each of those pies. In a zero-sum game, you simply cannot afford to reveal your position, to show your cards to your competition. And yes, Opaque Leader sees *everyone* as her competitor. Her team members are competitors for her job. Her peers and cross-functional department leaders are competitors for the attention, approval, and resource allocation from senior management. When you are in full competition mode with nearly everyone you interact with, it's hard to think about transparency as a positive virtue. It is more likely to be considered a symbol of vulnerability and weakness.

Transparent Leader, on the other hand, doesn't derive power from holding information. He doesn't even derive power from distributing information. He understands that the power lives in the information itself. By accessing information, inviting participation and input in problem-solving, and soliciting new information from those around him, Transparent Leader is enabling the power. The participants in his leadership style are empowered because of their access to a fully transparent process for solving business issues, for planning, for collaborating on customer solutions. Transparent Leader is not in competition as Opaque Leader is. He's working in a fully appreciative state, pulling in the best ideas on a continuous basis while leading the synthesis of those ideas and developing winning plans.

Transparent Leader has an abundance mindset. Sure, he thinks about his job, his career, his standing with senior management and his cross-functional peers. But rather than focus on the final score, Transparent Leader stays committed to the work. He understands that by creating the best environment for collaboration, he'll produce stronger plans, better results, and self-actualized teams. The final score in terms of his own career outcomes will take care of itself. Someday another person will take his seat, but he keeps moving in the confidence that by leading with a transparent style and an abundance mindset, his personal opportunities will keep coming.

Leadership habits about transparency seem to be hardwired in our managers. My own view, however, is that this competency, like all in this book, can be acquired. It takes a commitment to become more self-aware, avoid self-deceptive tendencies, and take risks when you have the opportunity by leading more openly.

TRANSPARENCY: APPLY IT

How do you develop a positive and transparent style? The simple answer is that you have to seek out opportunities to act as a transparent leader. It's one thing to be a completely open book, but that isn't always appropriate. There are clearly areas where you need to maintain confidentiality. However, on the great majority of business critical topics, I believe open management practices lead to better outcomes. Become the transparent leader by behaving openly in situations like these three below.

Identify situations where transparency is the difference between success and failure

We've already talked about transparency in the planning process. This is clearly an opportunity to bring more ideas together to expand possibilities and create better outcomes. But there are other situations in your role as a sales leader where you'll need to share information and elicit input from others. Generally speaking, any situation that requires brainstorming for new ideas is one where broader is better. Whether that is solving a customer problem, mapping out a project plan, or building a case for a pitch to senior management, you want more eyes and minds on your work. Many times you'll be trying to solve a problem that is in plain sight. Your familiarity with the situation can become a hindrance, as you are constrained by your knowledge of the factors you've become accustomed to seeing. Include others who have fresh eyes and limited biases to bring new thinking and lead you beyond the obvious options.

Personnel management is another area where the success and failure stakes are significant. Sometimes you need an outside perspective of a colleague, a senior manager, or a Human Resource expert to help your thinking about a potential employee or one whose performance has slipped. It's easy to become myopic when making hard calls on a current employee. You've become so accustomed to his style of working, you are blind to his behaviors that are actually harming your business. Bring in other observers to keep your judgment clear and make appropriate decisions about development or departure for these employees.

On the hiring side, it's common for managers to focus too heavily on the problems they are trying to solve today when screening potential employees. I've seen it time and again. An employee is terminated. Before hiring a new employee, the job description is updated and too much weight is given to addressing the problems caused by the departing employee. That over-emphasis on the behaviors that were absent causes judgment to swing like a pendulum to the opposite extreme. When a candidate seems to match those behaviors in their interview, they've got you. Make sure you have others in your hiring process who can make a balanced, unbiased assessment of the candidate. Transparency here can really help in keeping you honest about who you want on your team.

Be a transparency coach

Look for indications that your team members are operating with a scarcity mindset, and intervene with direct coaching. Is water cooler talk on the rise? Do you see signs of excessive meetings after the meetings where you're not part of the discussion? When you present information and ask for feedback, do you hear crickets?

You need to be an interventionist as soon as you have signs that sharing has dwindled or politicking has increased on your team. These situations can be caused by several factors. Perhaps you have been too opaque in the things you're working on lately, and that secrecy is fostering healthy paranoia on your team. Perhaps major changes are taking place elsewhere in the organization and your team members are fearful that another shoe will drop, on them. Or maybe you've got a few members on your team that are predisposed to living in a glass half empty world, and their pessimism has begun to take hold with your team.

I liked to use a few techniques to make sure I was on top of any transparency gaps on my team.

First, you need a few people on your team that you trust implicitly to clue you in to situations where you need to step in as coach. I'm not talking about snitches, and this is not playing favorites. These are people who are fully aligned to the business strategy and management philosophy you are pursuing and can identify small problems on the team before they become big ones. You need this inner circle of trusted advisers to help you lead proactively. This group is likely to be somewhat malleable, and you may find that different projects or initiatives require a different combination of these advisers.

Second, when it is time for your intervention, do it privately, and then publicly. Spend one on one time to get the person you are addressing aligned to your philosophy about the need for openness. Create a safe space for him by surfacing any anxieties he may have about giving up control over the information he is holding closely. Persuade him that power comes from sharing information, not possessing it. Once aligned, consider putting transparency behavior measures in his development plan, and support and recognize him when he exhibits desired behaviors. And then, yes, confirm these principles publicly to your team, without calling out the person you are coaching. Reinforce that all are expected to behave with transparency, then create an even wider safe zone for your pupil and a built-in support system for him to make the changes you are asking for.

Deflect praise and welcome conflict

Let's face it. You have a direct hand in some of the successes of your team, and you're barely involved in others. Assuming you are not overtly grabbing the credit 100 percent of the time, people above and around you will naturally associate the accomplishments of your team with your effectiveness as leader. Before straining your shoulder by patting yourself on the back, take a moment to think about that.

We'll talk about humility in Chapter Twelve. For now, remember that you'll get your due amount of credit whether you claim it or not. The role of the leader is to make the team she leads perform better than it could otherwise as individuals, and to do that better than any other manager. Your ultimate value to your organization lies in your ability to develop your people. You are expected to produce the next wave of leaders in your company, while you deliver today's requisite business results. You need to hire, develop, and support effective people who can take over your job. People who can take over your boss's job. The measure of your mettle is in today's success of your people, not in your genius to tell them how to achieve it.

Get close to the people who created the big wins and make sure you have an anecdote at the ready to describe their accomplishments, specifically and by name. Place your audience at the scene of their triumphs by being descriptive and animated. Your team members will show you their appreciation in their growing loyalty to you. Your company will recognize your dedication to producing people who can take over the reins in the future. When it comes time to list the names of people who can develop winning teams, you'll be near the top.

You may be asking yourself: *What about when there's a mess? When that big customer blows up at their salesperson because of a fulfillment error? When my team tried their hardest but missed the quarterly sales target? Even when the factors were out of my control?*

If you want to create permanent scars on your leadership brand, then throw others under the bus when things go south.

Believe it or not, this is one of the most common behaviors I've seen in managers throughout organizations. The ultra-competitive management culture that has emerged over the past thirty years or so, has flourished in companies that encourage a survival of the fittest mentality. Managers are challenged to succeed on their own ingenuity, in move up or move out environments. Talent management systems are designed to put permanent labels on leaders as either high potentials or no potentials. It's not surprising that managers in these organizations trade more paint jockeying for position than NASCAR drivers.

Instead, first isolate anything that is an individual performance problem. You need to address these situations with solid management practices and in keeping with your company's policies and procedures. Assuming though that everyone did their best and you just missed the mark, or the customer problem was beyond your sphere of influence, you need to step up and take the heat. Your job in these situations is to defuse the blame storm and step forward to acknowledge your ownership. Doing so places a bookmark on the problem so you can turn the page and begin working on solutions.

Don't succumb to the pressure in high stress situations by blaming others. Worse, beware of blaming others behind their backs during after action reviews when panel members are looking for a culprit. Take on the accountability and get others focused on diagnosing the deeper, non-personal causes of situations that didn't end up as planned. Take the high road and stay there.

Demonstrate that you and your team have learned from this situation. Impress upon your team that as long as they are putting in their best effort, you'll have their backs if things go awry. You'll find that your teams work harder and smarter over time, and commit to your priorities without hesitation. And your senior managers will view you as a leader with a sturdy backbone who is not fazed by setbacks experienced in the context of the greater mission.

There will be many more varied situations for you to exercise transparency as a compassionate leader. Make transparency part of your DNA. More than something that you do, it should become part of your personal leadership brand. Make it who you are.

Now you're leading your people openly with genuine empathy and transparency. Your visibility and involvement in situations are expanding rapidly. Your steady hand and calm leadership are now called for as you walk the path toward fully compassionate leadership.

Calm Steadiness

"Birds remain captive in the nets and traps because,
when they are entangled in them, they flutter and struggle
wildly in order to escape...Compose your judgment and
your will. Then quietly and gently pursue the object of
your desire, taking in order the means which are fitting"
— Saint Francis de Sales

Leaders who practice empathy and transparency are often well liked. But well respected? If you want to gain the trust, respect, and the following of your team, you must go further. Begin by modeling calm steadiness in chaotic settings. Be the person who continues to focus on the critical factors when it feels like you're drinking from the fire hose. The steady leader who can bring all her skills to bear to bring the team through the fire is the leader whose teams achieve sustainable success.

Put Your Oxygen Mask On First

Several years ago my wife and I were flying from our home in Pennsylvania to Florida for a getaway weekend. The kids were off to Grandmom's house and we were finally getting a short breather and a break from a long Philadelphia winter. We found cheap flights with a discount airline and off we went.

Approaching our destination, our pilot announced that we would be beginning our initial decent into Orlando and thanked us for flying with them. Seconds later the plane banked sharply to the left and dropped suddenly. I don't know if we fell a few hundred feet or a few thousand feet, but we were descending quickly. Oxygen masks dropped from above our seats. The packed passenger cabin let out one big collective gasp. In less than ten seconds, the plane leveled and stabilized.

Not a single passenger touched their oxygen mask. We had all heard the pre-flight instructions, and many had certainly been on an airplane many times before, but the masks hung in the air and swung with the movements of the plane. Everyone watched the flight attendant at the front of the cabin as he looked nervously out the window. Then after about twenty seconds from the moment the plane had recovered, he put his oxygen mask on. Immediately, all the passengers put their masks on as well.

I've always been puzzled by the reaction of the passengers, including myself, to what should have been an obvious signal to take a specific action. *Why didn't I put my mask on? Why didn't anyone put their mask on? Why didn't my logical brain override my emotional reaction to the situation? Why did we decide instead to play Simon Says with the flight attendant?*

In a crisis, or even in a triumph, all eyes are upon you as leader. You are always on stage. Whether you are addressing hundreds at a sales meeting, you're at a business dinner with colleagues, or you're with one other salesperson in front of a customer, you are being carefully watched. Your demeanor, your actions, and your speech are being chronicled by others as they assemble their perception of your personal leadership brand.

Recognizing your impact on others and demonstrating an ability to maintain an external calm steadiness, even when it feels like a swarm of bees is flying around inside your head, is essential if you are to create your intended personal leadership brand. You have to look for the telltale signals that it's time to turn off the auto pilot and take the controls from your reactive self.

CALM STEADINESS: RECOGNIZE IT

What Do You Do When Everything Isn't Wonderful?

Most new leaders can think of the first time they were faced with a career situation that prompted their fight or flight reflex. Your boss gives you an unexpected directive. Your heart rate goes up and your palms start to sweat. Your blood sugar drops and your hair stands on end. It takes every ounce of self-control you have not to overreact in the moment, to take that instinctive first step that might just be fatal.

First things first. Don't become robotic in stressful situations. Many leaders make themselves seem like a statue, appearing numb to situations that should obviously generate an outward response. Don't make this same mistake by going into emotional lockdown. You're human. Don't completely shut off your emotions, or even your natural reactions to events.

But the difference for you now as leader is that you can't always afford to react as freely as you might otherwise want to when you are surprised by something, whether positively or negatively. You need to keep your emotions in a channel.

When something great happens, you display measured joy, but stop short of temporary euphoria. When the train goes off the rails, your senses awaken appropriately to respond, but you don't show panic.

Treat these events simply as new information that will go into your thinking about your next series of decisions and actions. They shouldn't knock you off balance or make you stray from your ultimate course, which is to fulfill your personal mission and that of your company. Be careful not to create the perception that you have no reaction whatsoever, or you'll run the risk of being seen as aloof. Take startling inputs in stride, but don't let them break your momentum. Keep on walking toward your objective. Calmly. Steadily.

Here are three opportunities to recognize stress, manage your reaction to it, and assemble allies to create success in difficult situations.

Recognize your physical signals of sudden stress

The stress or excitement that comes from an unexpected stimulus generates a physiological reaction in your body. You aren't imagining it, and it doesn't only happen to you, no matter what your self-talk tells you. Learning to accept these chemical reactions inside of you can prompt you to respond in a way that doesn't put you in an uncomfortable situation.

In the winter of 2003, I had exactly one quarter of national team leadership under my belt at Green Mountain Coffee Roasters. After taking over interim co-leadership of the wholesale business with my partner James, things were good. We had taken over a business in decline, and for three months we had made enough of the right steps so that our VP had a tempered confidence in our ability to turn things around. But there was no question that we were still on probation.

On a mild Vermont winter day, I had the opportunity to speak at the quarterly company-wide meeting. The employees who worked in the headquarter offices and in our manufacturing and distribution facilities gathered for an update on the business. It was a big deal for me. A few hundred people were in the audience and it was easily the biggest audience I had addressed in my short tenure as sales leader. I had prepared for a few days for my presentation. It was merely fifteen minutes and a page of notes, but by now I had rehearsed my talk many times. I wanted to speak to the employees without notes, confidently assuring them that we were headed back in the right direction, and that I was the right leader for that challenge. I outlined our growth plan, thanked them in advance for their support, and assured them that my team would make them proud by representing them with integrity to our customers. Their customers.

The talk went great. Many approached me to tell me what a great job I had done. My head began to swell and my chest puffed. I was in that place. The place when you think everything is fine and there's not a cloud in your sky.

As everyone began to disperse, my VP congratulated me on my presentation and asked James and I to join him in his conference room for a meeting in fifteen minutes. No problem.

We strode into the conference room and were a bit surprised to see our VP of Human Resources in the room. Not shocked, just curious. We figured that she was there from a prior meeting. No big deal. Certainly nothing to be alarmed about.

Our VP started out by giving out copies of the P & L statement. As we would come to learn later, this was never a good sign. We would also later learn that a big chunk of his bonus was tied to the company's earnings per share metric. It wasn't the only thing he thought about, but good luck trying to make him forget about that, even for a minute.

After a brief setup for the purpose of the meeting, my fight or flight moment came.

Fire one Regional Manager. The one who manages your remote territories. Now. Don't overthink it. HR is here to help.

I honestly don't remember what else was discussed in the meeting. James was managing his own regional team, and I think he was told to let somebody go as well. But I don't remember. And I didn't care. I felt like a shovel had just struck me squarely on my forehead.

Where did this come from? Everything was going so well! Why now? Why this person? It wasn't fair. He didn't even know these people, barely knew their names. How could he decide who should get kicked out of the company? This was completely counter to the positive environment we were trying to create. It would be a punch to the gut for our new confident team. There's no way this could stand. I have to object. Put a stop to this right here and right now.

But wait. I was not yet standing on terra firma. I had been elevated to my role in something akin to a battlefield promotion. My boss had been fired, and I was the last best option left standing in the battlefield. I was still earning my keep. Still proving myself. In my mind, this was a test. *Did I have the nerve to fire somebody?* That was something I'd never had to do up to this point in my career. *Is that what this was about? I guess I would just have to prove that I was capable of that, and move on.*

No! I did not concur. But I was timid. I knew that with one misstep, my VP would start an external search for my replacement. After all, my title started with the "I" word. Interim.

I held it together long enough that the meeting ended and we agreed on some set of next steps. I left without throwing up on myself or tipping my hand too much that I was opposed to the directive.

I had stayed calm. And steady.

Luckily, nothing moves too quickly through Human Resources when you are terminating somebody from a large organization. From my perspective, this was great. I had an opportunity to regroup and assess things.

If letting my manager go was justified, then I could prepare exactly how I would approach it. On the other hand, the whole thing didn't feel right. My employee hadn't done anything wrong. Hadn't violated any policies. His business was trending in the right direction. I knew him to be a pretty good manager: he was an eight year veteran of the company with plenty of prior experience. He seemed to have the loyalty of his team and was strategic in the way he approached his business. He wasn't perfect, but he wasn't the worst either. Certainly not on the doorstep of getting fired.

As luck would have it, I had a managers' meeting scheduled for the week following my near panic attack, back at company headquarters in Vermont. I decided to make the case that we needed more time before we made decisions about cutting one of our managers. The team had recovered from a deep morale deficit when James and I were appointed co-leaders. They were rebounding nicely now and confidence was really building. There was genuine excitement about where we were heading. Firing one of the team's leaders would come as a shock and would surely be a setback to that progress. I worked up my courage and pitched my VP for another quarter or two so we could prove that our business performance justified our current structure and staffing plan.

My VP agreed, but there was a catch. He wanted each of the Regional Managers to present their business plan to him the following week so he could see them on their feet. It was his way of telling me that he reserved the right to be disappointed with the person he had in his crosshairs, and he would override me if necessary. I agreed and worked to prepare each of my managers for their presentations.

Following the presentations, my VP told me that the manager he wanted to get rid of was the best of all of them. He accepted my proposal to keep him on board and told me to keep my team moving. He said he'd look someplace else in the P & L for the savings he needed.

The moment in that initial meeting when fight or flight was all I could think about had passed. In the years that followed, I experienced that feeling again many times. The sensation is unmistakable. It is physical, emotional, all-consuming. I've been fortunate, though. I can't think of a time when I reacted impulsively in those moments, even though my internal voices were screaming at me to sprint in one direction or the other. Sometimes in both directions. It's important to recognize your own physical reactions to situations that challenge your steadiness as a leader. Stay calm and don't let the sudden stress overwhelm you.

Take control of the clock

I already talked about managing the clock in Chapters Three and Four. Particularly in threatening situations, gaining control of the clock is critical. In my example with my boss, I felt cornered with no time to collect myself. Somehow, perhaps simply because I was in some form of shock, I managed to defer the final decision to a later date. In that gap of time I could step away and think clearly, ultimately redirecting the situation toward an outcome I wanted.

A great example of when this tactic can save the day is when you are presenting to senior leadership, or even the CEO. When you are presenting to the CEO, and she asks you a question or challenges an assertion you've made, you'll feel a compelling urge to respond promptly and directly to that question. By all means, if you have clearly heard the question, and you have the home run answer ready, let it fly. Often, though, your CEO isn't intimately familiar with your business. She is merely immersing herself in your world for the fifteen minutes you are presenting to her. As a result, her question about your material is shaped by her incomplete understanding. It might not be as precise a question as you assess it to be. After all, she's the CEO, right? She's clearly got other stuff to worry about.

You, however, now have a racing heart and sweaty palms, because you've been called out to address her question. Chances are that if you answer right away, you'll answer a question you thought you heard, but not the one the CEO actually asked. You'll dance back and forth with answers and follow up questions while you clarify what each of you actually meant, and your presentation momentum will be in the ditch.

Instead, take control of the conversation cadence. Recognize the physical reaction you are having and prompt yourself to slow everything down. Ask a question instead of answering right away. Clarify her question. Guide your CEO's perception of you as leader. After all, you have the product. The answer. How and when you give that product away is under your control.

You can use this same tactic when you are taking questions for any other presentation, holding your staff meetings, or taking questions from customers. Call on your coping skills to own the clock.

Find a soulmate

As adept as you are at maintaining your calm steadiness as you navigate the ups and downs in your role as leader, sometimes you need to let it out. You've got to open up that pressure valve and let off some steam. More importantly, you need insights from others who are detached from the situation that has you in its grasp.

Find a small circle of people with whom you can work out ideas. People who are dispassionate about the situation you are trying to solve. These could be mentors, peers, direct reports, or even somebody outside your company. They must, however, be people you trust implicitly, who pose no inherent political risk to you as a result of the topics you share with them. Your relationship with these people should be explicit with respect to the fact that you are counting on them as your soulmate to help you think through difficult situations.

This might be one person or it might be a few. They should be intellectually and emotionally compatible to you. They must also demonstrate the ability to behave with a calm steadiness, understand the stakes you are playing for, and support your mission as an aspiring compassionate leader. My soulmates were diverse. Some were situational and others were global. In each relationship, I tried to give as much as I got.

CALM STEADINESS: APPLY IT

As with any of the competencies discussed in this book, your most resourceful self is ready to embrace your development in each area. In the serene moments that you are reading this book, you can visualize how you will become the compassionate leader you want to be. You understand the concepts, buy in to their value, and can't wait to get started on your way to becoming better.

But life is made up of more than just calm moments. Paraphrasing Mike Tyson's famous line, everybody has a plan until they get punched in the face. It's what you do next that determines your resolve.

You will stumble. It's OK. You will have situations when your best self doesn't come to the surface. I've been fortunate that those situations have been few and far between for me. Raising my voice with an employee. Countering a legitimate inquiry by a boss with a confrontational tone. Taking a defensive position when asked to explain why I missed a sales target. These will happen to you as well. Recognize them, take corrective action, and move on.

Pay attention to the way you embrace conflict over short and long-term horizons. Below are three pieces of advice to gracefully handle common situations you're sure to experience.

Accept direct challenges with an open mind

Guard against the fight reaction. There is nothing wrong with a good debate, and you should be the strongest advocate for your well-reasoned positions. But, you won't be right 100 percent of the time. Train yourself to participate in discussions and debates at a slower pace, and definitely at modulated volumes. This is difficult, especially on topics where you are likely to be the expert or ones that you are most passionate about. Keep a steady tone and cadence in these conversations, and don't get baited into behaving as if your back is up against the wall.

Avoid the tendency to take on a quiz show persona during debates on topics you know well. Don't talk over people or finish or correct their thoughts while they are still airborne. Slow down your reactive instincts. Use the time to hear out the other person and think about how to respond in a way that clarifies thinking and keeps them whole at the same time. I had a VP that I respected who was very good at this. He would allow the team to debate a course of action while he remained silent. Then he'd smile, tell us this was not a democracy, and would select one of the paths forward or his own previously decided course. We would rally behind that decision with good humor.

Put your shoulder into challenging situations

Your natural instinct is to avoid difficult situations in the first place. I wouldn't have chosen to ask for that meeting with my VP if I had known what I was walking into, right? Do I really want to pitch the CEO on my idea, and face his tough questions? That customer is furious with us, do I really need to be in that meeting?

The reality is that building your experience set in these settings makes you stronger. It makes you tougher. The more you see varied situations that cause you discomfort, the more you'll be able to see similar ones coming, prepare for them, and perform better. One of my closest colleagues used to tell me that if you're not experiencing some form of conflict in every meeting, then you are probably not talking about the right stuff. When I would accompany my salespeople on sales calls with angry customers, our team would meet for coffee first. Everyone was anxious. I would ask them what they thought was the worst thing that could happen to us. *Could we die?* Probably not. *Could we face physical injury?* I don't think so.

Would there be yelling? Maybe. By the time we walked through the possibilities and got to the business issues, we were smiling and eager to engage with the customer.

Nobody ever got hurt.

Develop long range calm steadiness skills

Beyond the day-to-day tactics and behaviors to guard against, you should be seeking out formal development of this competency. Enlist your Human Resource specialist or the person in your company that is your advocate for personal development. There are many fine leadership development programs available outside your company that can increase this particular skill. Another great option is to take public speaking training. For many people, public speaking is the number one generator of personal anxiety. Courses geared toward making students strong public speakers will undoubtedly help you with this competency. Even stronger would be to take an executive course in public relations, which builds skills to conduct media interviews and address questions on your feet calmly and coherently. This type of training will serve you well as you grow in your career and rise in your organization.

Standing with calm steadiness in your most stressful situations is an essential skill. The first time you demonstrate to your team that you are not fazed by a crisis, and continue forward with a purposeful stride, their respect for you will begin to grow. Create the time and space you need to make decisions that are consistent with your values. With your personal mission. Others watch you at all times now that you're the leader. Keep your cool and appear in control even in those moments when control is the last thing you're feeling.

Do you maintain a level persona? Do you treat all new inputs, positive or negative, merely as new information to help your decision-making? Calm steadiness is your gateway to establishing a learning orientation in your role as leader.

Continuous learning is the key to thriving in your fast-paced world.

TEN

Learning Orientation

"We become what we think about."
— Earl Nightingale

O n my first day in the corporate office after my appointment as National Sales Manager, I bumped into our CEO. "So how do you feel Jim, naked?" I gave a nervous response that I don't recall. But that was exactly how I was feeling. I no longer had air cover. I was exposed. I was excited about my new challenge, and I was terrified that I didn't know enough. Would my fear win this battle?

Learning As a Fear Countermeasure

I was never the best at cold calls. If I didn't think you wanted to talk to me, I really didn't feel comfortable about calling you or walking into your business to persuade you why you should. In fact, I could instantly imagine a dozen reasons why you wouldn't want me to bother you. I'm an introvert. An automatic minority in the profession of selling. When it comes to this essential skill in my chosen vocation, I'm a fish out of water.

On the flip side, I'm really good and energized when I can be the second man in, so to speak. Or third or fourth. In other words, if somebody else can set the appointment and be the front person in terms of setting the agenda with a client, then I am definitely the person you want at that meeting. Why? Because I simply love to learn.

I don't know how much time I'll spend on this Earth, but I do know that I'll spend every moment of it trying to learn new stuff. Asking, "What's up with that?" Chasing down answers. To me, life is about filling up that bucket of understanding until there is no more room, and then asking for a bigger bucket.

Learning is forward motion for me. But it is more than that. It's the way I overcome fear. I believe that if I keep a strong learning mindset, and pursue new knowledge and insights continuously, that I'll complete the task at hand, no matter how daunting. Then I'll spot a new, more energizing challenge just beyond the current problem. I begin without a notion of what that will be, but I've experienced the wonder of that discovery so many times, I know it will be there.

Here's an example.

By the fall of 2005, I was settling into my fourth year as a leader of a national sales team. I was hitting my stride. Then it happened. Boom. My VP left and a new leader from outside the company took over.

No problem. I've been through this drill before. My new VP would take some time to get acclimated, learn the flow of the business, and make changes only where there was a glaring problem. He certainly wouldn't look in my direction for that. Once he saw how smoothly things were running for me, he'd move on to another area.

Not exactly.

This would be my first close experience of reporting to a new leader who had a precise view of the way the sales world worked as a result of his prior experience, one who sought to implement a system he had come to believe in from the outside. His first day on the job, my fellow leaders and functional colleagues were meeting to finalize critical decisions as we kicked off the start of a new fiscal year. Among all the loose ends we were tying up was a big one, the sales team's bonus program. We were in a debate about how to structure the program based on our priorities for the year, how much weight to put into individual and team incentives, and how rich to make the program. It was my turn to speak.

Somewhere between the middle and the end of expressing my recommendation, a shoe dropped. My new VP stepped on my words and began expressing his views about how sales compensation works. Not his philosophy—the indisputable facts. They were divergent from my own view, built upon what I had seen work and fail at this company. But he had big company experience. Outside world experience. This was not the way he *believed* things worked, this was how they *did* work.

Discussion closed shortly after he expressed his views and asserted his decision. There was a new sheriff in town.

The new sheriff believed in a simple principle: When you are placed in command you take charge. Right away. You make as many decisions as you can as quickly as you can and you force others to try to keep up with you. When they can't and everyone spends their energy just chasing you and implementing all your decisions, you end up getting most of your agenda in place. When they catch up to you it is too late to challenge your approach, and you've created most of the organization and strategy you wanted.

It was a wakeup call for me. I started thinking less about standing out and more about keeping up. Changes kept coming, and my fears began rising. My administrative support team was commandeered. They would now report to my new leader along with support people from another team. My full P & L ownership changed. Now I only had ownership of sales and expenses related to sales. I lost ownership of payroll, marketing, and other discretionary line items.

While I was scrambling to adapt to my new reality, the biggest change came. Reorganization. He quietly announced to a core group that he planned to merge my sales team with a parallel team and divide the country geographically, east and west. My colleague who led that team and I were stunned.

My boss was direct with me. The reorganization plan would take six months to finalize and implement. At the end of that period he needed a leader west of the Mississippi River. He hoped that would be me, but if I wasn't willing to relocate, he'd be looking for a new leader out west.

I explored options outside my company during a brief period of discernment, then settled into the notion that I'd be starting a new challenge with a new team. I decided that Denver, Colorado would become my new home base.

I won't say that was the easy part, but it was straightforward. Sell my house. Buy a house. Move my family. Move my stuff. Tumultuous? Yes. Complicated? Not really.

The hard part was the reorganization. I had navigated significant change before, but this was different. It was comprehensive. Jobs were changing for 100 people. It was confidential. Leaks were strictly prohibited by our leader. It was structured. There was protocol. There was cadence. There was rhythm. I didn't know how any of it worked.

I started paying close attention and taking notes.

Balancing my personal anxiety as I considered changes to my own role and the impending transformation, I used the learning opportunity as a hedge against my fears. As a countermeasure. I kept telling myself that if I could get through this gracefully and learn as much as I could, the knowledge I'd gain would go into my quiver as a demonstrated skill for the future. I would know how to do it, and how not to do it.

Paying attention to what is happening to you while you're experiencing it is a critical skill if you want to become a learning leader. It's your opportunity to watch the movie in which you are starring, and give yourself an honest critique. You must become the best expert on the subject of you. Your commitment to continuous learning begins in your personal screening room and your subsequent scripts should exhibit your accumulated wisdom about you.

On your journey to become a compassionate leader, curiosity can be your best defense in times of uncertainty. The learning leader diffuses fear by keeping the words *I don't know* in his personal dictionary. These words enable exploration and permit vulnerability. Compassionate leaders don't avoid challenges even when they temporarily feel naked.

LEARNING ORIENTATION: RECOGNIZE IT

Commit to Learning When You Would Rather Move On

Sometimes opportunities arise from moments of fear and trepidation. Other times they are available to you while there is calm and contentment. In any situation, a dedicated learner looks for opportunities to acquire new wisdom. As leader this is a particularly important behavior for you to model for your team and your colleagues.

We've all had the experience of reporting to a manager that asked a lot of questions. But what kind of questions do they ask? Do they ask questions with the intention of catching us off-guard? Is it the pop quiz that is designed to keep us on our toes, and somehow teach us in our moment of discomfort that we should be aware of all factors at all times?

Or, do they ask us questions from a place of constructive curiosity? Do they ask questions for which they truly seek information, insight, and enlightenment? Are they asking the question with their arm around us, or with a spotlight on us? These leaders are selfless in their curiosity. They accept that not knowing the answers is not a sign of weakness, but not asking the next question is. Leaders who are always seeking the next question that can lead to further understanding produce teams that do the same. They produce teams who are always asking what else, why or why not, and what's next. Their teams perform better.

The need for a robust learning mindset shows up in your work as leader in many settings. Negotiating with customers, planning, listening to feedback, and cleaning up after a mess are significant learning opportunities for you. Here are four examples of situations when a learning orientation will counter your discomfort and carry you beyond your own expectations of success.

Customer negotiations

Suppose you are hammering out an agreement with your customer. Whether large or small, your negotiation is packed with pressures. You're trying to align on terms that benefit you and your company, while your customer is trying to do the same.

In an ideal world, we'd lay all of our cards on the table, find the points of overlap in our interests, and draw up an agreement that walks us right down the centerline of that road.

In most cases, though, there are factors that never come into play as negotiating points. These factors can be items either side holds close to their vests, or they may simply be things that nobody has thought about in the desire to reach an agreement. Embracing your role as a learning leader means you must devote energy to surfacing these issues now, during the negotiation, before they come into play later.

This is difficult. Protracted negotiations can wear you and your team down. Your customer appears to want to avoid beginning your actual business relationship as long as he can. Your clock is ticking loudly. You need to get past these tedious chess moves so you can begin engaging with the people in your customer's organization who can sell your product, and begin generating revenue. The voice telling you to accept the proposed terms is speaking more loudly than the one telling you to hold firm onto your positions.

You push on, and before you know it you've got a term sheet drafted that reflects everything you've agreed upon. You're confident that you've negotiated each point in good faith and for mutual benefit. And besides, if there are things you didn't think about, you'll be around to help work through any ambiguities once you've begun working together. All done. Sign here.

A learning leader calls a time out at this point. You ask the tough questions: *Is there anything we missed? Is there any scenario both parties can think of that would make either side want to break this contract? Not simply a dispute that would need to be worked out, but a true show stopper? An unforeseen event, a change in strategy, a competitive influence that might change everything between you and your customer?*

You must get these types of questions into the room when you are the lead on your company's negotiating team. You must ask, "What's the worst that can happen?" You then must prepare for that reality by addressing it in your agreement. Even if it is simply to add language that should it occur, the parties will work together toward a reasonable resolution, call it out.

Learning leaders keep not only their own eyes open, but they open the eyes of others in the steps of forging new business relationships like these.

Business planning

Any time I took over a business, and sometimes in the middle of my tenure as leader of a business, I forced myself to take a giant step backward. I used a variety of processes to assess what I knew and what I didn't know about the business I led. Early in my career these often took the form of a SWOT analysis or some other method of opportunity and gap assessment. As I became more experienced I went deeper. At Green Mountain Coffee Roasters in late 2012, I took over a new team that consisted of experienced employees to lead the company's food service sales channel. It became close to the ideal model for me on how to launch such an endeavor with the strategic curiosity of a true learning leader.

Inspired by my experience working under our founder and earlier CEO Bob Stiller, I chose to take a comprehensive and inclusive approach to building our strategic plan. Ten years earlier, Bob had introduced the company to a planning approach rooted in Appreciative Inquiry (AI). AI was different and ground breaking. It was positive. It was unbounded. It was inclusive.

AI was pioneered by David Cooperrider in the early 1980s at Case Western Reserve University.[9] Cooperrider originally interviewed doctors at The Cleveland Clinic to identify problems and issues in the organization's management practices. He was encouraged by his professor to focus on the positives instead. Cooperrider shifted his focus onto the factors that appeared to be life-giving to the organization. He later brought his approach to several companies seeking to solve problems related to efficiency, effectiveness, and growth. His work with these companies led to "dramatic improvements to the triple bottom line: people, profits, and planet." Bob Stiller introduced his employees to AI, and created a company culture that built upon the elements that gave it life.

I took a hybrid approach to building our first plan, keeping the core AI principle of approaching problems from the other side in play. First, I drafted a complete situation analysis of our business. Everything I knew from my experience and from available research resources. Time was of the essence for us. We needed as complete of an understanding of the current situation as possible to begin dreaming and planning. But we didn't have the luxury of commissioning fresh research to feed our thinking. We needed to have a very good, not perfect, understanding of the landscape.

It was a thorough, forty-page assessment. I asked the team and an extended group of stakeholders to read it. We printed copies and everyone carried a copy. We read it in our offices and re-read it on airplanes. We talked about it and learned it front to back and back to front.

Then I called a strategy summit meeting. The attendees were my team and our close cross-functional supporters across the organization. We met in an off-site location in Vermont during an early winter blizzard. For two days we dreamed, argued, asked questions, removed barriers, and identified gaps in what we knew and in our business. We generated proposals on the pillars of our strategy. We made decisions. Then we left and got to work.

We had a shared purpose and a common language and began to have successes. It started because we acknowledged that we knew a lot, and we didn't know a lot. We didn't get myopic about what we did know. Instead we dreamed about the possibility hidden in the things we didn't know, and embraced an inclusive process to discover them.

Planning cycles aren't simply the time to build upon your knowledge and experience to articulate your intended path. It's your opportunity to clear the brush and see the trails that you haven't yet taken, or even create brand new ones. You can't do that if your fear of the unknown convinces you that there are no new ideas.

After a crisis

One of my favorite bosses used to have a great saying. He would tell me in his comfortable southern style, "Jim, it takes one Oh Crap to wipe out ten that-a-boys." But he didn't say crap. Usually that came just after I had wiped out another ten that-a-boys. He was a great leader though, and taught me much in my pre-leadership development years.

When you experience that fecal fan collision, your first instinct is to clean up the mess, get the heck out of there, and try to forget about it. It was the same with me. I minimized the immediate damage to avoid any long-lasting scars, I kept my head down for a while, then I got to work on putting ten more wins in the plus column to erase everyone's memories of the situation and my role in it.

My colleague James helped me to change my perspective about these situations. He liked to use a metaphor of rounding a corner and getting hit in the head with a shovel. Pleasant, huh? You have to survive these events, there's no question about that. If you don't, there's no sense in trying to learn lessons from the disaster. But when you get smacked in the forehead, you must ask the question, "What the hell was that?"

As we discussed in Chapter Four, The U. S. Army calls these after action reviews, and many companies have adopted formal processes for examining how major projects were executed, whether they were done well or poorly. The organizational learning is intended to support better execution on the next similar initiative. In my experience, the teams that did the work on the project are usually either too tired from the execution of the prior project or already immersed in the work from the next project to put proper energy into the review. The reports go into a drawer or onto a hard drive, and are unlikely to be resurrected later for their intended benefit.

If you are caught by surprise by the outcome of any consequential initiative that you thought you had prepared for properly, you should consider that a shovel strike. Rather than following the instinct of getting as far away from the situation as you can as quickly as possible, go closer. Time to get curious.

James and I used to sit back in our chairs, let out a big exhale, and ask, what happened? What did we miss? Why didn't we see this coming? Because we operated with fairly low ego, we didn't let our bruised feelings or our pride get in the way of real understanding.

Sometimes we spotted a critical factor we had ignored that now seemed to have been in plain sight all along. Or we identified a surprise influencer that we had discounted earlier, but who proved to be the difference maker in the outcome. Or a tactic that we were personally enamored with had no positive effect, or worse, undermined our efforts and created a catastrophe. It's true that diagnosing the patient after he's dead is probably easier than when he's sick, but sometimes you don't see the sickness. We tried not to move onto the next surgery until we found out what we did wrong on the last one.

Your after action reviews don't have to be complicated, but they do need to be thoughtful. You'll only learn if your mind is wide open and your ego is checked. Failure to learn from your mistakes, especially your big ones, has the potential to stall your leadership momentum.

Approach the shortfalls you surface with curiosity and be visible doing that. Your ability to face fear publicly will empower your team to do the same, no matter how weary they may be at the end of the project.

Get feedback, then take action

It is likely that in your role today you have a mechanism for getting feedback about how others view you. If you include a self-assessment as part of your annual performance review process, ask your team and close colleagues for inputs. These can be helpful, but sometimes people pull back on being completely honest because of your work relationship. Then, your supervisor will give you a review, but will probably focus on specific behaviors against your agreed upon goals or development plans. Again, helpful, but probably not game-changing feedback for you.

My best experiences with receiving very honest and incredibly helpful insights on how I impact others have come within the context of facilitated 360-degree feedback instruments. I've had the opportunity to do this several times in my career. Sometimes these were anonymous and other times not. Surprisingly to me, one that was not anonymous was the most informative for me and the most impactful on my career. The results literally changed my life.

I wasn't surprised when I heard that people wished I would speak up more. I had already heard that I was on the quiet side. It was the *reason* they wanted me to speak up that surprised me.

People told me they wanted to hear from me earlier in group discussions and meetings where we were debating strategies. They respected my opinion, my knowledge of the topics. But the reason really grabbed my attention. They wanted to hear what I thought earlier, so *they could complete their own thinking and form their point of view on the subject.* They appreciated my insights, but because my words came at the end of the discussion, they didn't get any real value from hearing from me. They wanted to know what I thought sooner so they could decide how *they* should think.

This came as a complete surprise to me. Once I received this feedback, I thought completely differently about my participation in all types of meetings. My perspective did a 180 after my 360! I had been afraid to take risks until I understood that I would be helping others and myself if I stepped out more. It was no longer about managing my own risk by not saying something dumb too early, and waiting until I was 100 percent sure of myself. Now I saw my participation as an enabler for others to build understanding and contribute more.

I countered my fears by learning this key dynamic about how I was perceived by others.

The lion's share of my personal growth came from my openness to receive feedback and my hunger to learn more about myself. If you choose to focus on one behavioral change from this chapter, make it your commitment to develop a healthy self-awareness from insights gained through the eyes of others around you.

LEARNING ORIENTATION: APPLY IT

So how do you become a learning leader? How do you become oriented toward gathering insights, developing wisdom, and applying your refined thinking in your mission as compassionate leader and effective coach?

The ability to develop a learner's mindset is not found in a seminar or training program. The desire to learn, not just from the technical manuals, comes from within you. It is a discomfort about what you don't yet know. An uneasiness about thinking that things are getting too easy. An anxiousness when you realize you don't have enough healthy conflict going on at the present moment. Or the panic that sets in when something catastrophic happens that you didn't see coming.

As with many of the essential skills in this book, start with small steps and accumulate them to form a mindset for helping yourself and others. Commit to behaviors that support your orientation to learning. Involve allies in your learning and let people around you know how they can support you. Inspire the same behaviors in others and support their development. As you develop your learning orientation and model the mindset of a thoughtful leader, take these four opportunities to build a strong foundation.

Model your behavior with your team

Be open and demonstrate how you approach business planning, personal development, and crisis management. Show your team that while you have learned much along your path to this point, each experience, whether a setback or a triumph, is an opportunity to add to your knowledge. Impress upon your people that having good answers is great, but asking the best questions is even better.

The leader who leads with curiosity and well-intentioned collaborative energy to pursue the truth, has the permission of her followers to be imperfect. She involves others in her quest, shares the journey with them, and celebrates alongside them when answers are discovered. She reminds them that the journey continues, points to the next mountain peak, and keeps the team moving.

Go public

There's no better way to generate support for something you are passionate about than to tell others and ask them to help you. Building a vibrant support network around your quest to become a learning leader and leading learner is a good idea, if you're serious about it. I'll come back to the abundance versus scarcity question from Chapter Nine. The leader that relentlessly pursues wisdom, only to keep that to himself, discourages others from volunteering information and testing hypotheses publicly. Leaders who perceive that their power grows by holding information, undermine a learning culture.

Keep the words *I don't know* in your vocabulary. These three words make you stronger, not weaker. Bring your team with you along your learning journey, and if they find a path you can't see, accompany them willingly.

Go public with your learning mission and lean into opportunities to build up the people around you. They'll support you in return and make you stronger than you can become without them.

Find a mentor, be a mentor

I've talked a bit about the need for mentors here and in other chapters, and it is an essential ingredient for leaders who want to continue to develop personally and rise in their organizations. But when it comes to developing a sustainable orientation toward learning, it really is a must. There is something unique about the capability of two people with this type of relationship to go deeper on questions and surface robust solutions together.

The mentor is the person who can be the objective observer when you can no longer rise above your scene to observe it from the outside. A true mentor helps you clear the snow, the debris, the fear, and your head. He gets you thinking clearly again, with energy to go back and bring your best self to the situations that dominated you a few hours earlier. While it may be awkward to *formally declare* the nature of your relationship, you have an understanding. You wonder together about possibilities, and you do so without the risks of sounding dumb, being lost, or being overwhelmed.

If you step outside your personal space and take a look upon your relationships, you'll likely find that you already are a mentor to at least one other person. You'll see the person that comes to you to talk stuff out and confides in you specifically for her most challenging dilemmas. You didn't make an agreement with her. Your role as mentor is not explicit. But it's there.

Take the next step. Make it explicit. Tell that person that you are there to support her, and invite her to come to you with her most challenging business situations. Create a safe space where she can process theories, hypotheses, incomplete thoughts, and dumb ideas. Allow for some unconstrained venting when that needs to happen. Keep it all secure within the relationship you have with her as mentor.

You'll be surprised what happens. The benefits of playing both roles in a mentoring relationship will sharpen your broader skills as a compassionate leader. You'll strengthen your ability to recognize business problems that call for your hard skills, sharpening your judgment and identifying your own gaps for development. You'll get great practice on your softer skills as you mentor another person. Instilling calm and inspiring clear thinking will make you more capable of self-managing your way through your own crises.

Don't overwhelm your team with training

One of the most predictable actions I've seen in new sales leaders, myself included, is to launch a giant training initiative shortly after taking over the reins of a new team. Almost any initiative he recommends that appears to have thought and discernment behind it, will get the OK of senior management and will garner considerable resources. Chances are that no other senior leader is close enough to the team and current conditions to refute the recommendation anyway, and the new leader usually starts out with a pretty lengthy leash.

Soon after the training is completed, the new tools begin to go stale. Since the deliverable is checked off the leader's list, the incentive to assign ownership to keep the lessons fresh is missing. There is certainly no more money to spend with the outside trainer to keep everything updated and continue upon the path that the leader started. Of the 20 percent who bought into the program, about half keep using the techniques they learned. But across the remainder of the sales team, most go back to their old habits.

What's worse, team members have now branded the leader in a negative way. This training was not put in place to help the team. It was implemented to polish the new leader's brand. Confidence soon erodes, and the team is once again at the loading platform for a train ride to leadership change.

Training for training's sake, or to check a personal performance measurement box, is a waste of time. Yes, there are good uses for group training, but only for concepts that are completely new or when you are trying to shift accepted practices from A to B. Genuine effective training is personal. It occurs at an individual level. Clusters of individuals may need similar training, but it's up to you to surface individual needs and group people together if that is the case. Don't make the mistake of starting a big learning initiative and dropping that on your team because you think you're supposed to do that as leader. It may not create the results you expect.

These and other guideposts will help you make smart choices when it comes to you and your team's learning path. The key is to learn. Always. If you are feeling comfortable about what you know, stop. Disrupt your comfort by accepting that you don't know enough. Then ask why and learn more. That's what a learning leader does. The first time you demonstrate to your team that you are not fazed by a crisis, and continue forward with a purposeful stride, their respect for you will begin to grow. Behave this way consistently, and your team will learn to stay in step with you.

Now, you've got it all together. You practice genuine empathy and you allow your team to see you openly. You accept challenges with a steady hand. You learn from everything you do and apply the lessons to perform better. But what happens when it all goes wrong?

Let's now see how well equipped you are to bounce back from your setbacks.

ELEVEN

Pragmatic Resilience

"Above all, don't lie to yourself. The man who lies to himself and listens to his own lie comes to a point that he cannot distinguish the truth within him, or around him, and so loses all respect for himself and others."
— *Fyodor Dostoyevsky*

As a rising leader, you're in for a wild ride. You are likely to experience the highest of highs and the lowest of lows in your journey guiding others through the thrilling world of sales. Your ability to keep a realistic outlook about your experiences will indicate how well-grounded you remain. The speed with which you resume your balance, your pragmatic resilience if you will, is the mark of the leader who can remain present and effective. A story about an event that occurred early in my leadership trajectory reminds me today about the need to embrace reality and keep moving forward.

Coming in Second

In the summer of 1999 I had several years of pretty solid sales success and two years of competent regional management under my belt. My star was rising and I was building fans. Then, suddenly, an opening in the sky: National Sales Manager. The big chair was open for bidding.

I couldn't believe my time to confront this opportunity had arrived so quickly. My career goal was definitely upward mobility. Keep climbing toward the top until I couldn't climb anymore. It was a natural reflex to begin thinking about myself in that role I currently reported to, seeing myself in that chair, making the tough calls.

There were strong suggestions that the company would look outside for a replacement with a pedigree. That's not uncommon. Behaviors seen as missing in the current occupant of the role tend to drive hiring managers to look beyond their own walls to find candidates that appear to already have them.

I decided to go for it.

I didn't mail it in, either. I prepared. I studied. I took an outsider's view of the company, my division, the team I would manage. I knew the factors currently affecting the business. I knew the good and the bad. I knew the pulse of the sales team better than anyone else. Management could see the sales numbers. They also knew the good and the bad. I put on management's goggles and looked at the business from their vantage point. I thought about what was broken and how I would fix it. I thought about who I would involve in finding solutions. I built my case about the potential outcomes of the change I recommended. I articulated the intended impact to the team, the division, and the company.

There were three rounds of interviews over six weeks, with panel sizes growing and the number of candidates shrinking with each round. I came prepared to each round. I brought materials into the meetings, I made strong cases for my views, and connected well with the interviewers.

In between the interviews, I worked my internal network. I let key influencers know that I was competing for the job. Their conversations with the hiring team would surely have an impact. It's one thing to directly persuade a decision maker that you are competent and qualified. It's quite another if they hear that several times from other voices whom they trust. That's how risky decisions get made. That extra validation takes the risk out of the decision and diminishes the attractiveness of alternative choices. I knew that was particularly true in my company. And I knew that picking me was a risky decision for the hiring team.

The interviews were held at our corporate headquarters in Vermont. When I traveled in for interviews, I used my spare time to drive around neighborhoods. I drove past schools. I imagined myself moving into the community. I even bought my wife some candles for the beautiful home we were sure to buy. After all, once I was selected there would be no time to waste. I wanted to get to work on making a difference.

Two weeks after the third round of interviews, when I knew it was down to myself and an outside candidate, my VP called me in my home office in Pennsylvania.

"You did a great job in your effort," he said, "But we have decided that we do not have a qualified candidate for the position. We'll be continuing our search for an outside candidate."

What?

Not only had I not been successful, but they weren't selecting anyone. I lost. To nobody?

The brief call proceeded to its conclusion. We said goodbye and hung up. Thud. My head hit the desk and I let loose. Total disappointment. Tears. I was completely floored. *Was this it? Game over as far as my career with the company?*

I regrouped a little over the next few days. I thanked the hiring team for their consideration of me. I asked for feedback on what I could have done better, or what I could work on for the next opportunity. I reiterated that I was committed to the company, and I wanted to contribute to help the organization win in any way I could. I expressed my support to the success of the selected candidate.

But I was seriously wounded. For the better part of six months I hid my true feelings. I went through the motions.

What had happened to me? Other people try for promotions and I didn't notice any of them feeling as devastated as I had when I didn't get the job.

I had a serious deficiency in what I now call pragmatic resilience. I didn't maintain a practical perspective on my candidacy, on the motivations of the hiring team, of their pressures to effect change in the candidate selection process. I thought everything was going my way because people were being nice to me. Well, people are usually nice to you. It's easier than being blunt. I couldn't see beyond the smiles in the conference rooms.

Because I wasn't keeping it real with my understanding of my chances, I found myself in a deep emotional hole that was difficult to climb out of when the news hit. For months, it was easier for me to stay in that ditch. Luckily for me, few people could see I was living there. I did recover, but with greater pragmatic resilience, I would have bounced back onto my feet much sooner.

The good news was that I did make a good impression. When the time came a few years later that the position reopened, senior management looked to me to help stabilize the business. The same VP who had delivered that difficult news became my biggest advocate in the organization.

Going all in is the only way when you are stretching to achieve a significant goal. You have to fully commit and not hedge your bet. But keeping a realistic perspective is essential to recovering when the goal is not achieved. It is the key to resiliency, and a must for the rising compassionate leader.

PRAGMATIC RESILIENCE: RECOGNIZE IT

Surviving the Big Ones

Interesting bedfellows. Pragmatism and resilience. Why the fusion of these two skills, each of which should be in your repertoire independent of each other as an effective leader?

Salespeople and sales leaders are optimistic by nature. We have a belief in the possibility of the future. We hear the word *no* more than almost any other profession. Some say we are predisposed to see the silver lining in any situation. That may be. More likely in my view is that we become conditioned to see our way through situations that would be discouraging and immobilizing to people who don't share our experience. A salesperson picks herself up after getting knocked down. She keeps a short memory about setbacks and keeps on striving. That's resilience. That's not usually our problem.

Pragmatism is the enemy of optimism. It says that of all the potential outcomes of the action I'm about to take, the most likely one is in the middle of the range of possibilities. It lies somewhere between complete failure and wild success. Pragmatism tames optimism. Lowers expectations. Preserves feelings. Keeps us safe. Unfortunately, pragmatism also undermines inspiration, imagination, and creativity.

Pragmatism assumes a manageable level of disappointment in our results. It modulates our effort and commitment to stretching our ability. Pragmatists don't push themselves to forward frontiers, they wait for the railroad to be built.

One of my favorite movie scenes that illustrates the conflict between resigned realism and pragmatic resilience is in *Apollo 13*. Following a terrifying explosion on the spacecraft, the mission faces a series of challenges in their quest to return safely to Earth, any of which have the potential to end in death. In one of these, while the vehicle is drifting off-course, flight director Gene Kranz is advised that the crew must execute a manual and unguided rocket burn of the lunar landing module engines to get back on course and make it home. Kranz asks the Grumman technician whether the vehicle his company designed and built is capable of the maneuver. The technician tells Kranz that it wasn't designed for that purpose. Kranz pushes and pushes the technician, who maintains his realistic stance and sticks to that fact. Finally Kranz explodes and tells him that he doesn't care what it was *designed* to do. He wants to know what it *can* do. What is it capable of?[10]

Kranz knows this machine was built for a different purpose. He understands the reality, but he doesn't stop there. He doesn't limit his energy, effort, or imagination of potential outcomes by stalling out on that knowledge.

As leader, you must inspire movement. You don't do that by keeping everyone safe. You can't stand still and avoid risk. When faced with situations with ranges of potentially positive and negative outcomes, you have to fully commit to your chosen path, and be ready to pick yourself and your team up if it goes bad. My own profound disappointment was a wakeup call for me. I knew that going for it was the correct strategy, but I was taken aback by my inability to see and accept the real picture that was before me. I hadn't developed the dual mindset of pursuing an optimistic outcome, while preparing myself to bounce back up if I got knocked to the ground.

You'll face this strange dichotomy as leader during times of change, significant losses, and your big career calls. Consider these three situations where you may be tempted to hedge your bets and play it safe, but where you must commit to going all the way with a genuine intention to succeed.

Major organizational change

Whether we're talking about a reorganization of your company or division, or perhaps a major new initiative where your team will have to embrace new learning, you'll face a unique challenge. Who can cut the mustard? In the new reality that will be implemented, which team members will swim and which are sure to sink?

I've seen this thinking take hold quickly in times of major change initiatives. Time is of the essence. The voices attempting to influence and guide your management approach to implementing this change will be many and loud. *We can't coddle people. Either they get on board and embrace the change we are making or we have to replace them and move on. We can't be holding hands here. Everyone needs to clap on or clap off. Don't overthink this. In any project as complex as this one you can expect 10 percent of people to fail. In fact, Bill and Sue and Frank probably won't adapt to the change, so we should just cut them before we get started. They'll only slow us down.*

You can follow the conventional wisdom and nobody will fault you. But conventional wisdom isn't necessarily wise, and it's only conventional because a lot of other people have copied it. Think for yourself. Consider the example of Ernest Shackleton, captain of the *Endurance*, and famed Antarctic explorer. Shackleton led his men on an exploratory mission to the South Pole. The crew was caught by surprise by adverse conditions, and the ship became trapped in the ice. While waiting out the situation and hoping for the ice to subside, the opposite occurred. The ice began crushing the ship. Shackleton faced a crisis and a daunting new mission: march across the ice hundreds of miles to civilization and survival.[11]

In today's management environment, Shackleton would be excused, even lauded, for letting go of the weaker crew members who might hold back the rest of the crew, and threaten survival for all. Pragmatism dictated that Shackleton make this judgment and save as many as possible, accepting a smaller number of human losses.

Ernest Shackleton thought differently. He committed to the survival of each person, and the new mission was built around that objective. Everyone had a role in the mission to achieve 100 percent survival. After two years on the ice, the entire crew reached civilization and survival. Against the longest of odds, Shackleton had accomplished the impossible, not the merely practical.

You see, there is a funny thing that happens when you agree to accept minor losses on the front end of a major initiative. Your mindset becomes self-fulfilling. You create the losses you envision. You have already banked them. Even if you think you are doing your best to avoid them, the fact that you've already made yourself comfortable with accepting some small degree of failure, ensures that you'll experience those losses. Furthermore, you won't be putting your full energy and focus into your project with a total success mindset. Gene Kranz was famous for barking the phrase, "Failure is not an option," during the Apollo 13 crisis. He didn't say that a little failure was acceptable, or if he lost one out of the three men that would be OK.

Unless you commit to all of your team members at the outset of a significant change management project, your project will not fully succeed. It is only when you commit all the way like Kranz and Shackleton that you'll produce the optimal results. If you do suffer losses, you'll know that you gave it your best effort. Losses will be difficult, but you'll be buoyed by the fact that you put your whole head and heart into trying to avoid them. Resilience will come quickly and you'll be ready for the next big initiative.

Significant business losses

There's a catch-22 in the business world and especially in the selling profession. The great thing about big customers is that they really move the sales needle. Big acquisitions of new customers or major expansions of existing customers can put you and your team over the top against your annual sales targets, and result in individual financial rewards.

The flip side of that coin of course is that when they drop you, and drop they will, big customers disproportionately affect your performance on the negative side. And because there are fewer big ones than small ones, the chances of replacing that business quickly are slim. When you lose a big customer, your sales year may effectively be over. You're not making bonus and neither are the people directly connected to that customer. You have a lot of explaining to do.

You strive daily to add new business, new customers. When you start to gain momentum developing your customer relationship, you agree on growth strategies to expand your business. Your key customer grows and grows and eventually represents a more and more significant portion of your sales and revenue. Or perhaps your persistence at winning that already large prospect finally pays off. You begin doing business and before you know it a large portion of your eggs are now in her basket.

The reality is that many customer relationships change or completely end over time, because of a variety of factors. Some factors are in your salesperson's span of control and some are not. In either case, the impact on you as leader and on your career momentum can be significant, even terminal. Your ability to face reality through the course of the relationship and your ability to regroup after a big loss say a lot about you as a sales leader.

I've won and lost many major customers over the course of my sales and management career. I knew that each big customer relationship was only as strong as our performance as a company, and my performance as the face of my company. I also knew that we were always one big problem away from losing that customer.

Of course, you could always hedge your bets. Work only with small and medium size customers. If you lose them you'll be able to cover those losses with an acquisition push, as long as your sales pipeline stays filled. But its likely that your company won't be satisfied with that type of slow, incremental growth. Your executive leadership wants big wins. Headlines.

When a customer drops you, it's time to demonstrate your pragmatic resilience. Educate your team on sales lead times and the difficulty of timing customer acquisitions. Make sure they remain on great terms with the departing customer, and be ready to step back in if they find that the grass isn't greener with their new supplier. Wind down the business gracefully, and make concessions where reasonable to leave a favorable impression. Then, keep calling on the customer. Most do not do this. They treat a big customer loss like a death. Stay positive, cultivate the sales funnel, and be ready for the unforeseen opportunity when it appears.

Of course, in some cases, the worst happens. A large customer moves on, and your sales year is shot. Your salesperson is crushed. No bonus this year. He pleads his case for an adjustment. That's another topic for another book, but let's assume that's not an option. Depending on how many people were tied to the account, you've got a real risk of a large number of people mentally checking out for the rest of this sales year. They'll restart their motor near the end of the year and work on next year's bonus. But the sales process doesn't work that way. Sales aren't something you turn on and off like a light switch. I've seen many a salesperson derail sales performance with this thinking. Your role as leader just changed.

You can only expect resiliency from your team if you model that behavior yourself. It's easy to head for the house of suffering with your team after a big loss. But there's no value in that commiseration. Accept reality but don't become satisfied with it, and be prepared to bounce back up and restore optimism with your team. Leaders who can do this distinguish themselves and gain the confidence of senior leadership, who will believe you cannot be deterred by any challenge.

Big career decisions

OK, this is the big one. When do you decide to stay or jump? To climb or exit? These are the big calls you make for yourself in your career journey. The risk-reward equation looms large in these situations. Depending on where you stand on your career arc, this decision can be easy or very difficult.

You'll face career choices that have higher risk than reward. An opening appears that you're expected to apply for, but it isn't something you really want. The jump in pay is nominal. The responsibility load is much greater. The prospect for success is poor, or it doesn't look like a viable stepping stone to future growth. Perhaps relocation is involved. You've got to take a realistic assessment of this type of situation and make a big decision. Your options are to go for it even though it's not that attractive, decline the opportunity and face the possibility of being stamped as not promotable, or recognize that the opportunities with this company aren't there for you, and decide to exit. Each choice has risk.

I had a business school professor in the mid 1980s tell me that I should plan on changing companies, or at least jobs, every three years throughout my career. This was the philosophy that was taking hold at the time. Keep moving. Advance your career by changing teams. Don't bother trying to stay loyal to a company that isn't going to return the favor. The biggest companies were adopting a survival approach to management development. Train young managers in several different disciplines across the organization. Then give them a team and a P & L and let them flourish or flounder. If the former, their ascent up the organization would be nurtured. If the latter, they were discarded and replaced by the next class of management trainees who showed up from the feeder business schools.

Though I didn't realize it was happening at the time, I had unwittingly followed my professor's advice. I spent my first twelve years after graduation working for four different organizations. It wasn't my plan. It just worked out that way. I had gained a diverse set of experiences but had no real identity since I was constantly reintroducing myself to new environments. I was certainly not on anyone's leadership development track. There were no opportunities for advancement because I hadn't been in one place to build a meaningful track record of accomplishment. I did good work, went home, and showed up the next day.

Then I joined Green Mountain Coffee Roasters and my career changed. Before long I was advancing, taking advantage of opportunities to stretch, grow, and progress in the company. There was really no question about whether or not to go for the opportunities that showed up, because the prospects of succeeding easily outweighed the risks of not succeeding. But that won't always be the case in your career.

Pragmatic resilience is a great way to approach your career choices. Imagine yourself in the new career scene after all of the available decisions. What will it be like to work there? How will people view you, respect you? How will you view yourself? How much time can you imagine spending in each of these scenes before you are frustrated? Can you see your next opportunity more or less clearly from that standing point? Visualizing yourself in that picture will not only help with your decision, it will also help you get a head start on adapting to your new reality. It will build your resiliency.

All my career moves were easy in comparison to my last one: my decision to leave my company after twenty years.

There were a few items that had become non-negotiable. I wanted a seat at the strategy table; a real seat where I could steer my business with my years of accumulated knowledge, experience, and insights. I wanted to execute a strategy that had my name on it. It would have other names on it as well, but I had to believe in it. Lastly, my work had to be important and leading to the next scene, as it had in my entire career. I didn't want to be trapped in another person's movie.

At a company-wide sales conference in the fall of 2014, it hit me. None of my non-negotiable items applied. My seat at the strategy table had moved to the back of the room as our company had transformed into a more traditional corporate model. The strategy I had signed my name to was replaced with a contradicting strategy. Finally, I couldn't see the next scene anymore. I could only see the scenes that others were creating. I was in them, but my speaking lines were dwindling.

Before the final day of the conference I literally spent an entire night awake thinking about my situation. When you decide you want to do something different with your life than what you're currently doing, and you're sure about that, you want to start the other thing right away. I decided I wanted to do work that was fulfilling and helpful to other people with my life. In the morning, I started the conversations than began a process leading to my departure. And a new start as a writer.

The risks of that decision were significant. I left a good job where I was well compensated for no job. But I was faced with making a real judgment and being honest with myself, so I fully committed to my decision. Each day I continue to respond to that challenge. It was the best decision and the hardest decision I ever made in my thirty-year career in business. I couldn't have made it without pragmatic resilience.

PRAGMATIC RESILIENCE: APPLY IT

Compassionate leaders lead with their head and their heart. To lead only with your intellect is to miss the human element in the interactions you have with those you influence. To be guided only by your emotions is to forego the judgment that comes from applying your technical wisdom. There must be a balance.

To consistently demonstrate pragmatic resilience and develop discipline in your decision-making style, you need practice. You need exercise to develop the muscle memory so that it becomes your natural inclination. As you rise in your role of leadership, here are three simple steps you can take so you'll be able to develop the habits you need to build this competency.

Inform your team

Your employees need to know that you are the leader who encourages agile decision-making. When you keep your team in the loop, they take on acceptable levels of risk. They want to produce positive results as a member of your team, and they step out enough so you have a unit that pushes the limits in a healthy way.

Let's face it, your main objective is to grow your business. If you can't accomplish that you're headed for a job change. You need your team to stretch their thinking and their actions to find the growth opportunities in the marketplace. That can't happen if you are hiding information or playing the blame game after a decision that falls flat. Create your team culture around striving for more and supporting the team when they stumble. That culture will become your foundation for your intention to lead with pragmatic resilience.

Train your manager

The closer you get to the top, the more likely you are to encounter managers who have less tolerance for bad decision-making and significant losses. Whether you work for a public company or a privately owned one, the stakes for missing a target get much higher at the top. At this altitude, surprise bad news can be hazardous to your career health.

A very important element to prepping your boss is to define the space you have to recover from setbacks with her. You have already created that safe zone with your employees, but let's assume your manager hasn't come to you to tell you to go out there and fail and it will be OK. You should initiate this conversation. Be as direct as possible. Tell her that two things are going to happen as you manage this business you've been assigned to lead. You'll win some and you'll lose some. You need to be very clear about her appetite for losses. How much can she stomach and still allow you the time and latitude to correct? How big of a loss can the company tolerate before it has a negative effect beyond her ability to manage collateral damage?

It's essential that you come to an understanding on these limits. Your survival meter should go red anytime you see the possibility of an outcome that could cross over this line. Remember, one of your responsibilities as leader is to make your boss successful. It's not your only duty, but it's near the top of the list. Keep her informed, get her involved, and share the ownership of your decision. She'll give you air cover in case things go bad, and quite possibly suggest options you hadn't thought about.

It's one thing to keep an agile mindset on recovering after you've made a decision. But if you haven't defined a safe space above you to do that, your ability to take those risks can be limited, and dangerous.

Keep score and pick your spots

Do you remember my boss who lived by the ten good moves to one bad move ratio? Telling me about his rule of thumb was really his way of pointing me toward the scoreboard. I don't think he had a tally about me on his whiteboard, but he was definitely keeping tabs on his people in some fashion. Your manager is keeping that tally on you, and so are your people.

The leader who takes too many risks and fails, well that's easy. You lose the following of your team. It can be nearly impossible to win them back. They don't trust your judgment or your acumen. They stop bringing you situations, they chat it up at the water cooler, and begin to freelance. Your business is effectively no longer under your supervision. But even if you take risks and win your share, you may fail to build a sustainable reputation as trusted leader. Taking too many chances, even if you seem to have the golden touch, may not distinguish your leadership abilities in the eyes of your team. You'll be seen a lucky gambler. Your team members may believe that anybody could do your job, themselves included. They lose respect for you and see you as temporary occupant of your role as manager.

Use discretion and keen judgment about risk and reward when making a decision with the possibility of unknown consequences. Be pragmatic and resilient. It's fine to have a mindset that you can regroup from any eventuality, but you don't want to live your life climbing out of ditches. Accumulated perceptions about your leadership chops may just leave you in that ditch one day.

Think about your own scenarios and be honest. Take risks knowing that you'll be able to recover from any difficulties your decision creates. Smaller situations call for this competency, but the big ones will test you. Tackle those and you'll know how to meet any challenge with confidence and commitment.

Each day is a new day for you as leader. Your understanding of your reality and your learning as leader has expanded as a result of the prior day's experience. Today is the next step on that journey. Approach today with pragmatic resilience. Be prudent. Be decisive. See where your decision leaves you tomorrow and go from there. And then keep going.

Just don't let all that success go to your head.

TWELVE

Humility

"If anyone would like to acquire humility, I can, I think,
tell him the first step…is to realise that one is proud."
— *C. S. Lewis*

I am under no delusion about the challenge of this final competency of the compassionate leader. There's a reason you're reading about it at the end of the book instead of the beginning.

You arrive here with a firm grasp on eleven competencies designed to solidify your compassionate leadership brand. You are strategic and have business acumen. You execute and deliver intended results. Your judgment is sound and you make the tough calls with a long range focus in mind. Your relationships are mutually respectful and open. Those around you appreciate your steady hand and your appetite for learning from your shared experiences. No matter what setbacks you encounter, you bounce back and keep on your journey. But there's just one more thing.

Now you must let it all go.

The business world is intensely competitive. Smiles and handshakes belie the political calculations lurking just a few layers below the surface in professional relationships. Sometimes those measured tactics are not hidden at all. This is a place where finding humility is akin to finding treasure at a garage sale. Even if you think you see it, you'll need an expert to help you determine if it's real and why nobody else spotted it.

According to Merriam Webster, humility is "the quality or state of not thinking you are better than other people."[12] It would have been easy to skip this virtue in my profile of the compassionate leader. Leadership is a contact sport after all. In order to move up you need to climb over another person. Peers around you are making the case they are better than you to be in line for the next promotion. Leaders above you are separating you from their level by holding information, leveraging their seat at the strategy table, and garnering and protecting the resources that keep their power intact. Humility in the workplace is surely a pipe dream for you, isn't it?

No. Humility is the skill that activates all the others.

You are like the captain of a ship. You set the course, monitor progress, and call for navigational adjustments. You stand high on the bridge as the face of success or failure. But deep down, you know that the crew is carrying you to your destination through the hard work they do.

It's easy to stand on that perch and accept the gaze of admiring onlookers with false pride. To employ the self-deception that tells you how deserving you are of the praise of others for a job well done, for stunning business successes. Others can't see the crew working down below the bridge. Your fellow managers and your higher ups see the nameless faces of your team at the annual sales conference, but organization charts don't have enough room to list your team members by name on the printed page. They are listed by functional title or grouped by their sub-team as an anonymous unit. There is little time or energy for your peers or superiors to dig deeper to see who is making your ship move through the water.

Let's Be Friends

I could tell a hundred stories about how humility was absent during my career. Situations where politics and power clouded collaboration. Situations where I wish I had had the clear-sightedness to see through the motives of people around me and call out their unbridled self-promotion at the expense of others. There are plenty of these stories. If you want a story about unfairness and power politics in the workplace, you can surely find one in your own experience.

I could also tell you a story about when I was the model of humility in my actions in a given situation. How I brought a selfless mindset to a situation that needed my genuine and full engagement as a humble person to help my team solve a complex problem. I'm sure I have a few examples of when I demonstrated true humility. But I'm human, and almost any example I give will have moments of self-absorption and thoughts of self-promotion. Perhaps even actions where I jockeyed for a favorable position with my own interests rising above all else. I'm not perfect.

Following my completely sleepless night at our company's annual sales conference, I had an awakening. I wanted to do something very cool with the rest of my productive life, and it wasn't a continuation of what I had been doing for the past three decades. Time for me to leap.

I am fortunate. My career in business has been fruitful. I have been successful enough to allow me the freedom to make such a career choice, a choice to explore and discover what my biggest contribution can be in my time here. It's a gift and I don't take it lightly.

After thirty years, and twenty with one company, I decided to step away permanently. Although it felt like a secondary consideration, I wondered what would happen to my relationships. In what ways would they change after I was gone? How much did that matter to me?

I knew I needed to decompress. I decided to goof off for a few months, let all of the work stuff drain from my mind, and then get busy on deciding what was next. Great plan. I love to ski and I love to golf, so I thought I would spend time becoming great at both of these activities with my newfound freedom.

As part of my plan to let go, I decided to lay low for a while and disconnect from people following my departure. I needed the space and certainly didn't want to keep processing the work while I was trying to clear my head. But I also didn't want to cloud anything for my former co-workers. I wanted them to get on with their work lives and I also wanted to give new leaders the space to lead without the voice of Jim in the background.

When I decided to begin making contact again with my friends from work, I intentionally wanted to change one thing. Even though I considered myself to be a humble person when I was on board, my relationships were primarily defined by our mutual status in the organization. Manager, employee, colleague, department head, project team member, supervisor. Any friendships that I had developed, had first passed through these filters.

That part was over now.

Since I've left the company, I've been able to step through that doorway. Friendships are real. Despite our prior work status, I've gotten closer to many of the people I worked with on a level that doesn't depend on a defined hierarchy. Just people.

For some it is harder. The hierarchy still lingers. As I thought about this, I began to observe other post-work relationships. I've seen people who were friendly at work completely break those relationships when one or both people were no longer at the company. Perhaps the organization chart was the only thing holding them together. Perhaps the person whose name was printed higher on that chart still believed they were superior. There are other factors like time and distance that limit continuation of the bonds. We say goodbye and let go of people many times in the course of our lives. Why is that?

The situations I see and personally experience where the hierarchical status remains after the defined relationship has ended are particularly troubling to me. We have opportunities to connect with a limited number of people in our lifetimes. Gifts. When we approach each of these encounters with a judgment about who is better, smarter, more worthy of courtesy or respect from the other person, we waste that opportunity. We waste the chance to connect equitably with another person. We dismiss the possibility that through that mutual connection, both may grow.

Humility is a double-sided coin. Heads says you are no better than anyone else. Tails says that nobody else is better than you. We're all even. Some are smarter, some are faster, and some are stronger. All are equal persons. To ignore this is to accumulate regrets in relationships, experiences, and choices. To understand this is to walk freely through life with compassion and vulnerability.

Use humility as your cloth for wiping clean today's whiteboard of regrets. Did you handle a situation poorly in your past? Were you unfair to an employee during a time when they struggled? Did you grab credit or deflect blame when doing the opposite would have been more appropriate? Activate your humility now by paying attention to the following suggestions and keep them with you throughout your journey.

HUMILITY: RECOGNIZE IT

Turning Down the Spotlights

Ego lies in wait for the leader. He stands ready to accept praise, press the flesh of admirers, and is poised to accept the next compliment and the next promotion. Ego knows that these are the moments when careers are made. He knows that the natural anonymity that falls over your team like a dense fog fixes the spotlight upon you as a solitary character, ready to embrace the moment, and shines upon your personal star. Ego is ready and waiting for this opportunity.

You've seen it. You've seen the person who seizes these moments. Who steps away from the company of his team to bask in the light of praise and accolades from above. The one who gives token credit to his faceless team, because it sounds magnanimous, only to call for the floodlights to shine upon him brightly thereafter. It's hard to fault this person for grasping the opportunity to surge ahead of the pack. After all, in today's competitive corporate environment, you've got to make your own breaks if you're going to keep climbing higher. Don't you?

Living with humility will be come your biggest challenge as a leader, especially if you're effective. It is a natural thing to want to succeed, to want recognition. Of course you want to advance in your organization. You want to keep stretching your skills, capabilities, and your ability to effect positive change.

What is the balance you need to strike? Can you serve both masters? Can you stand above your team in the spotlight *and* engender their loyalty?

Understand that ego undermines loyalty. Humility is not only more admirable, it is also more practical. Humility supports delegation and managerial efficiency. When you claim the credit for work completed, you assume more personal ownership over that work. Your team begins to withdraw and you are left holding the reins. People come to you to solve things instead of the experts on your team. Before you know it, you're deep in the weeds at the expense of your other priorities.

Ego also forces you to keep score. Players who play the game with too much focus on the scoreboard ignore the necessary tactics of successful execution. If you are spending all your time sorting out your people, you'll have little time to guide them toward victories. Lead with an open heart and the score will take care of itself.

Humility must become part of your DNA, your wiring, your internal code. It must be intrinsic to how you operate. That's not a simple thing. It's completely normal to want to be told we've done a good job. It's a basic human need to receive praise. To be loved. How do you make humility and ego compatible? The secret is to place ego in service of humility.

Make your self-esteem dependent on your ability to keep your self-perception level with your perception of others. Accept praise, then balance that praise genuinely with the people who are just as deserving of it. There are group settings in your role as leader where you'll have the opportunity to do this; below are four for you to consider: sales calls, presentations, training activities, and recognition occasions.

Joint sales calls

Your presence on customer visits and top-to-top meetings with your salespeople are opportune moments for your head to swell and your ego to take center stage. Everyone in the meeting, your team members and the customer's team and leader, expect you to take command. If you're not careful, you'll assume the helm and undermine the objectives your salesperson planned to achieve during that meeting.

A short story from my experience illustrates the perception that accompanies you as the presumed power player in these meetings. As Regional Manager in the Spring of 2001, I had one-up managerial responsibility for our largest customer, a convenience store chain in Pennsylvania. I accompanied our Area Manager on all calls to the customer's corporate headquarters. The head buyer was a particularly tough cookie. He completed master's level courses on how to harass vendors, and he was good. On this particular visit, he was working on getting his costs lower, and I was in his cross hairs. As a friend of mine liked to say, he gave it to me up one side and down the other. When it became clear we weren't going to satisfy him, I called an end to the meeting just to preempt being thrown out.

Four months later I had been promoted to National Sales Manager. We paid our favorite buyer another visit. He couldn't have been nicer to me. He offered coffee. He offered pastries. We joked about current events. He still wanted help on pricing, but his delivery was more cordial. Executive to executive. We couldn't quite deliver what he wanted, but we smiled and agreed we would keep looking for opportunities to make him more profitable with our products. We left the meeting.

I wasn't expecting that treatment. I was the same person. Did he realize that? I was torn about how to react. But I had made a big mistake. I had accepted the attention. It felt good to be treated with respect. To be treated like something of a big shot. I hadn't made an effort to defer the attention to my team members, the people who owned and supported the relationship. I forgot about the humility. Now I was leaving a meeting with a person I might see once per year with a bunch of follow up actions I shouldn't own. But now I did.

Support your team and let them get the attention. They're the ones who are going to deliver value to your customer. Use your humility to make their relationships stronger by putting your full support behind them, instead of jumping in front of them. You'll be more effective and efficient as their leader, and they'll want to support you even more.

Major presentations

As you progress in your leadership roles, you'll likely have numerous opportunities to present to groups. Whether at your sales conferences, company meetings, annual kick off events, or industry speaking engagements, you'll get your fifteen minutes, or longer, of fame.

Leaders should be *of* the team as well as *above* the team. You must be present with your team, supporting, coaching, counseling, and teaching them. When the work is happening, you need to be available and accessible to help them get over the top and win. Once they've won, you need to slip away. I'm reminded of the 1980 U. S. gold medal Olympic hockey team, as portrayed in the movie *Miracle*. After defeating the Soviet Union team in their epic match, as the team was ecstatically piling onto each other on the ice, head coach Herb Brooks was nowhere to be seen. He had slipped away to a hallway underneath the seats of the arena. He enjoyed a quiet moment of satisfaction alone while his players celebrated wildly and deservedly at center ice.[13]

Your speeches and presentations are your opportunity to shift the focus away from you and onto your team. If you are celebrating a great sales year, thank your team. Recognize individual accomplishments. Put names on the anonymous faces that are driving your company to succeed in the marketplace. If you are predicting a successful year, call on your team members by name and articulate what you and the organization are depending on them to deliver. Then stand assertively and proclaim that you'll be there to fully support them. If you're speaking to an outside organization, avoid the temptation to use that speech as a personal public relations venue. Speak with a mindset of service to the greater group. Invite them in to join your cause, whatever that may be. Getting others to remember your message is more important than getting them to remember your name.

I've seen this at work. I've shadowed a colleague who spoke at trade shows on topics designed to benefit the industry at large, and was later invited with him into a competitor's booth to talk about their latest products. I've presented awards to fellow employees, then been approached by a senior leader who asked how he could support my own success. I've listened to talks about social responsibility in business, then sought out more on the topic to round out my own perspective and share my learning with my team. When you bring humility to these settings, everybody benefits.

Training seminars

As a leader, you'll initiate or implement training programs for your teams. In today's continuous learning business cultures, chances are your company will encourage this as an annual occurrence.

First things first. If you are requiring your full team to go through any comprehensive training program, you need to be there. It doesn't matter if it is sales training, education on a new computer application, or some other functional skills development. If you are requiring everyone to go through it, you should as well. I'm not talking about sitting in the back of the room, looking at your smartphone, and ducking out of the room every twenty minutes for a call. Be the best student. You should know the material better than anyone and be able to apply it and teach it when you're done.

OK, now that I have you in the room, please don't be this leader: the one who has to appear like this is old hand to him. The one who answers the facilitator's questions before he finishes the question. The one who challenges each section of each module with your real world example from your vast experience.

Sure you can participate: after all, I just told you to be the best student. But don't dominate. Your role, in addition to that of student, is as assistant facilitator. Pay attention to the room. See who's struggling, who's not engaged, who's surging ahead. Connect with the training team during breaks and point them in the direction of these hot spots. You are the primary sponsor, and you own the success of the program. Use your humility to apply the highest leverage by helping the facilitators and the students work together effectively, without hijacking the room.

After the training is completed, you must become Chief Implementation Officer. Incorporate the learning into daily behaviors, and reinforce them by prompting their application when you are with your team members. If the training was technical in nature, get your hands dirty. Use the new computer application in real world situations. Identify the situations that create frustration for you, and recognize that your team members are probably experiencing the same thing. Diagnose problem areas and work with the core team to fix them.

The time immediately after a training initiative is completed is the time most lose motivation to bring the lessons to life. That's your job no matter how unglamorous. Stay humble and make sure it happens.

Sharing accolades

I talked about the public settings when you should be deflecting praise onto your people, but what about when nobody's looking? It's just you and your manager having a conversation. She congratulates you on winning that big customer. The company really needed that business. And you did it. Way to go.

Individual recognition is the highest source of job satisfaction. It's more important than salary, bonuses, commissions, and awards. The act of another person thanking you for a job well done is the form of recognition that sticks with you the longest. Its absence causes people to leave jobs and companies. So if that's the case, it's perfectly natural to bask in that warmth, right?

Here as well, seek to deflect praise onto your front-line people who delivered the results. Of course you helped. You may have even carried the ball across the goal line when the team got a little stuck. Your boss already knows you're playing a big role in the success of your team, so don't keep the praise of this moment all to yourself. Call out your team members whose fingerprints were all over the triumph that has your boss excited. Then take one more important step.

Ask your manager to directly contact the individuals on your team responsible for this accomplishment and thank them for their great work. Yes, the recognition she tried to bestow on you felt good. But when she steps into your organization to recognize individuals personally, they will feel superhuman. They'll want to create another success just like this one. Your team will start a pattern of success and a tradition of winning. That's why you're in your role to begin with. A little humility in these situations will dramatically increase your value with your team.

HUMILITY: APPLY IT

My advice is simple. Find humility in your organizations, in fellow leaders, and in your personal relationships, then emulate those examples.

Look for organizations with a humility culture
Find the companies, established and emerging, that build their organizations around a sincere belief in the worth of their people. Companies that walk their talk. You'll need to look hard and pay attention, because these companies' spokespeople may not stand up in front of microphones and talk about their humility culture. Find out what others are saying about them. Take notice of their actions in the marketplace. Watch them when they are faced with a crisis.

These companies are led by their people, not by a single person or a personality. They solve problems because groups of employees pitch in, without an expectation of individual recognition. In these companies, you are more likely to hear peers recognizing and praising each other than an individual at the microphone bragging about a success. When there is a problem, somebody comes out of nowhere to make the diving catch for a colleague. They fix the server on the weekend. They get the big order out the door. They show up to help at a customer event on their personal time. These companies are emotional. They are inspirational. Look for them.

Find the humble leaders

Who are the people in your network who obviously lead with others front of mind? I can name the managers and leaders who have been in my life that led with humility, and the ones who led with ego. It only takes a moment to decide on which side of that fence they stood. Get close to the leaders in your life who are humble. Watch them and model their actions. Construct your moral compass in a way that you can be that model for future leaders you are developing.

Be cautious about emulating the humble leaders in celebrity circles. It's easy to think of famous personalities in business, or sports, or government, that appear to demonstrate traits of humility in the way they lead others. Unless you have the unlikely opportunity to really get close enough to know these people personally, be careful. You get to see a very small percentage of that person's full humanity. Chances are good that you're seeing a practiced and polished version of that person. It may be the genuine person that you're seeing, but it may not. Don't be fooled into imitating a person to whom you can't get close enough to verify the image you see.

Find humility in everyday life

There are people all around you, outside of your business life, who live a life of humility and fulfillment. They are not doormats. They simply accept the equitable relationships in all aspects of their lives and they meet others where they are, without assumptions about comparative status. Everyday people think of others first, while not discounting their own value.

These are the people that sometimes cause you to tell yourself how you wish you could be as generous and humble as they are. Stop wishing. Find the humble people in your life. Get close enough to them so you become what you wished you could be. Walk with them.

Humility is hard. It takes courage. It is counter to many signals you receive daily, about how to be your best and make sure everyone knows it. About end zone dances and self-promotion. About trophies, money, possessions. There's nothing wrong with these things. But if you're the only one staring at your trophy case, it can get pretty lonely.

Humility isn't just *necessary* to become the modern compassionate leader. It is *essential*. Even if you are already great at the first eleven competencies we've discussed. The leader who wraps his works in a blanket of ego simply looks like every other leader out there who puts himself first over others. For that leader, yes, it is only a matter of time until he rises to the level of his incompetence. Until he hits his head on his personal career ceiling and begins a slide back down the ladder.

That's not you.

Keep a crowd of people around you when you succeed, and blend in as a person no better, and no worse, than they.

Compassionate leaders like you do that.

PART III

Conclusion

THIRTEEN

Becoming the Modern Compassionate Leader

For the past thirty years or so, the conventional wisdom about management development theory has been in conflict with the notion of compassionate leadership. Thousands of today's managers have been manufactured in organizations that have infused them with contradictory values. Trainees enter corporations with pedigrees from the most prestigious business schools. They take a fast development track and gain management training in multiple functional disciplines in a relatively short time span. They settle in with one of these departments where they assume command and effect immediate change. After a two- or three-year reign they are on to a new assignment and more responsibility, either within their organization or with an outside firm.

For a great many leaders in organizations today, tenure is not a word in their vocabulary. They do not stay in any one role for more than a few years. Relationships have a singular role: upward mobility. Deflection of accolades onto others is rare, unless of course they are buttering up the boss. Competition is intense. There are only so many seats at the top. When the music stops they can't take chances. Or prisoners.

Chances are good that you work in an organization like this. That's because this culture has been in development since before most people who currently work in corporations were out of high school, perhaps even before you were born. Companies that demonstrate a more compassionate culture are few and far between. Their stories are attractive because of their novelty.

It doesn't need to be that way.

Proponents of the conventional approach to management development would argue that it has produced unprecedented economic success and financial benefits for individuals and companies for decades. I don't quarrel with the economic achievements. I do believe however that positive and progressive corporate culture has been a gradual victim to the mentality that producing wave after wave of alpha managers is the only path toward business success. Though rarer, there are examples of companies whose nurturing culture correlated with impressive sustainable performance. Doing good and doing well are not mutually exclusive in business.

GETTING STARTED

Who Are You?

I've seen two types of leaders rise up through organizations.

Leader A has dominating strengths in a few specific competencies, such as sales or operations, but blind spots in others. He tends to over-play and over-promote his strengths. His successes are trumpeted. He develops a brand by being great at a few specific things based on his publicized achievements. People who see Leader A from afar may assume he is good at everything based on his persona. People who are close to him however see the gaps and experience the consequences. Leader A tends to approach new challenges by going to old pages in his playbook. He is convinced that if something worked once it will work again. He is focused on the opportunities above more than the realities below. He becomes detached from his organization and pursues initiatives that are not operationally feasible. Ultimately he reaches a point where his gaps can no longer be ignored and he is replaced by a new leader, who has a mess to clean up.

Leader B pays attention to the things she doesn't know as much as the things she does know. She manages with a curiosity that allows her to embrace new knowledge. She understands that an organization works best when all functions are operating effectively, and she works to understand each function. She spends time with people across the organization, shadowing work, building relationships, developing a personal appreciation for the complexities in the business. She asks how she can help out. She listens. She learns. Leader B has a general manager mindset and grows into a belief that she has ownership of success in all the parts of the business she touches. Even as she rises in an organization, others are drawn to her because of her desire to keep learning and improving. Leader B is quietly inspirational. She builds teams that sustain success. She leaves organizations in better condition for the next leaders when she leaves.

In my experience, Leader B begins with a philosophy that learning doesn't end because you've been promoted. Early in her career, she dedicated herself to improving every day, to paying attention to her knowledge gaps, by exercising acute self-awareness, and seeking truth.

You are the culmination of actions and reactions you have made in the course of your life to this point. That's who you are right now. Today and each day that follows this one, you have the opportunity to make changes that will define who you will become. Tomorrow, just one day from today, you will become a different person. A different combination of accumulated experiences and insights that combine to paint the portrait of you. That will occur again the following day, next week, and in all the remaining days of your life.

Each day we learn. In my life I've made it my daily goal. Even on my worst day, when everything seems to trip me up, when my resourcefulness is rolling around the bottom of the deepest valley, I learn. One thing. Something. I gain understanding about something that I didn't possess the day before.

This is the gift of becoming. I receive this gift every single day—do you also receive it? Before I close my eyes at night, I get a chance to reflect on who I was that day and how I'll add that to my understanding of myself. When I sip my coffee the next morning, it is with me. It is now one of the pieces that make up who I am at that moment.

This book is my gift to you. My wish is that the stories, lessons, and guidance I've shared inspire you to make big changes in your career and your life.

So where do you start? Which is the most important of the twelve focus areas?

You need all the tools in this toolbox. Each one. Hard and soft tools. Technical and emotional tools. My advice to you is that you select one or a few skills that you want to work on. Take an active approach to seek out mentors, training, and participatory experiences to build your strengths across these competencies. As you think about prioritizing your development, consider these key questions about each of the twelve competencies we've discussed.

Strategic thinking

Key questions:

> ➤ What is your current authority over strategy?
> ➤ Do you have sole authorship? Are you a core strategy team member?
> ➤ Do you have input to strategy without decision authority?
> ➤ Are you only responsible for executing someone else's strategy?

Your degree of authority will help you prioritize your learning on this skill. The closer you are to the authorship role, the more urgent this competency is for you. Get started right away. Secure solid professional training and get a hands-on tutor within your company who is expert at writing strategy or executive coaching. Get others involved and vested in your rapid development in this area.

If you are currently responsible for execution of someone else's strategy, take a longer view. Find an accomplished and respected leader in your company who can mentor you on strategy development. Get a seat in the back of the room at key planning meetings. Get an advocate in your continuous learning department who will facilitate your opportunities to shadow key strategic work in your company. It's important to do this work inside your company, versus relying only on external training at this stage. You need to learn your company's norms and process as much as you need to try on your own strategic thinking cap.

Functional competence

Key questions:

> ➤ Is your organization a customer-driven or sales-focused company?
> ➤ Is it a process-driven company?
> ➤ Is your company focused on executive leadership development?

Prioritize your learning here based on two factors: your company's orientation as a firm, and your own known shortfalls in expertise across the four functional competency dimensions.

For your personal skills, you'll find a wide variety of external training resources across all subjects. These are the core topics that business training programs cover, and have been refining for years. Work with your manager to identify one or two skills you want to develop and enlist them as your sponsor for the outside training you need.

For skills that are well aligned with your company profile, inside training is preferable, if available. The subjects that are compatible with your company's personality are likely the ones where in-house programs will be strongest. In addition, there is a cultural element to this training because it is so integral to your company's identity. You need to learn these subjects in your organization's unique lexicon with any proprietary nuances baked in. Outside training will miss that part.

Productive intent

Key questions:

> ➤ Do you understand your company's productivity culture?

> ➤ Are deadlines respected and achieved?
> ➤ Do you work in an environment where due dates come and go without consequences?
> ➤ Are you building a tradition of timeliness?

On the personal level, good time management techniques are indispensable. Long ago I sampled several workflow management systems and picked one that I've stuck with for years. You must do the same. Don't fall into the trap of switching to a new system because you're not getting more timely on your deliverables. Pick a system and stick with it.

Organizationally, learn the systems that dominate scheduling and work completion in your company. You'll need to work within these systems in order to understand how they support the productivity of your company. These systems should be application-based and capable of driving behavioral change. Mastering the applications is straightforward and essential. Understanding and influencing informal behavioral systems is different. Drive reliability of deliverables by learning, mastering, and advocating for best practices around getting work done in your team and your company.

Sound judgment

Key questions:

> ➤ How are decisions evaluated by the organization? By teams?
> ➤ Is there an honest feedback mechanism built into your processes? Your performance reviews?
> ➤ When results of decisions are disappointing, what are the consequences?

It's easy to understand if your judgment is sound or not. You're there. You see the results and the reactions of those around you. Personal improvement in this area is more likely to come from staying engaged and communicating openly before and after big decisions. Importantly, don't let more than a few bad ones pass before you're soliciting feedback assertively. Remember, too many swings and misses and you'll lose the confidence of your team.

In your organization, you must understand risks associated with your judgment calls. Get a few senior leadership allies on your side who can coach you through tough calls. You may feel that you know exactly what to do in a given situation, but unless you really know how your executive team reacts to bad news, you'll be on an island. No matter your confidence in this area, you need sounding boards and backstops from up above.

Long range focus

Key questions:

> ➢ What is the relationship between short and long range goals in your company?
> ➢ Is there a quarter to quarter emphasis, or does the longer-term mission supersede that?
> ➢ Does your sales department talk more about orders than relationships?

Understanding your company's orientation about short or long-terms sales results is a critical factor for this skill. If you are in a pressure-packed environment where closing the quarter above plan is paramount, you can't appear to be dreaming of the future. That said, all companies have some notion of where they want to be in five or ten years. Your job is to be educated on short and long horizons so your activities and outcomes are congruent to both. Become astute enough at this so your priorities and timing are not fighting those of your organization.

On the personal side, I highly recommend developing your visioning muscles. A key to long-term planning is to see a future state and imagine yourself in that scene. That is the foundational step that precedes assembling the pieces and people you need to get there. Look for outside training on visioning for business success. I believe this learning works best in a professionally facilitated environment with interaction with other students.

Managerial courage

Key questions:

> ➤ How are you perceived by others when it comes to taking risks?
> ➤ Do you share your views early or do you play it safe?
> ➤ Do colleagues look to you in tough situations, or do they work around you?
> ➤ How often does your boss ask you what you think about a business dilemma?

While this is mostly a "you" thing, it's important to gauge how your organization values risk-taking. Do senior leaders extend a hand when there is a setback or do they reach for a stick? Make sure your boundaries are consistent with your company's cultural norms around risk and reward situations.

Managerial courage requires a dedicated coach to help you up your game. Chances are that your Human Resource or

Continuous Learning team has a resource available for dedicated one-to-one leadership coaching. Access that person and begin a sustainable relationship on this development area. Make sure that includes a robust 360-feedback tool so you can get a clear read on your perception as a courageous leader. Then work with your coach on any areas where you have a shortfall or where you overplay this skill. Repeat the assessment every one to two years to track your development.

Empathy

Key questions:

> ➤ Do you think mostly about consequences for you or for others in your business interactions?
> ➤ Do you ask what keeps your customer, employee, or senior leader up at night?
> ➤ After an interaction is completed, do you ask what happened or do you move on quickly to the next task?
> ➤ In meetings, do you finish sentences for others in an attempt to answer questions you're sure about more quickly, or do you let the answer emerge?

Internally, understand how your company values empathy. Look at things like employee benefits, the way problems are solved, how plans are built and implemented. It's easy to see empathy in a company's policies and practices, or to not see it. Influence your organization to the degree you can by asking the why and why not questions when you encounter low empathy in the way it conducts business. Drive your structural development by stimulating new thinking to help you and others grow.

On a personal level, the joint sales call is a great place to begin a dialogue with your people that centers around understanding your employee and the customer as whole persons. The extended side by side time in these settings should be your platform to explore your application of empathy with rich, open-ended questions and discussions. It's often easiest to build this skill in post-interaction conversations by questioning what just happened in your shared experience. Access outside training and independent study to spark your thinking about becoming more empathetic.

Transparency

Key questions:

> ➤ How do you view the power equation about holding or releasing information?
> ➤ Are the stakeholders around you more opaque or more transparent?
> ➤ Do you struggle with managerial courage? Does that difficulty spill into your comfort around behaving transparently?
> ➤ Can you imagine what would happen if you acted with complete transparency? Or if you were completely opaque?

Let's start on the personal level. Transparency is an individual trait. You should be able to quickly identify where you stand on the opaque-transparency continuum. You should also see where your employees, colleagues, and senior leaders stand. Begin by establishing your own goals about how transparent you wish to become. Are you going to let it all hang out or will there be limits? Begin by working with a few trusted individuals. Select people who are on both ends of the scale and express your desire to behave with more transparency. Make agreements that you'll challenge each other when you are not forthcoming enough, or when you're playing it safe with information that should be shared. Expand your circle gradually as you increase your comfort level in sharing information freely.

At the organizational level, understand the lines between transparency and confidentiality. If you're not sure, ask the question. *Can this information be shared or does it need to remain confidential?* Get very clear on these protocols and ask each time new information reaches you if you are unsure. Beyond those items that must not be communicated broadly, challenge senior leaders with your insight about why sharing a particular piece of information with your team would support better execution. *Would the additional context help front-line decision making? Would involving more people in strategic information aid development of future leaders?* Learn where the communication boundaries are in your organization and engage in exploration of moving those toward more transparency.

Calm steadiness

Key questions:

> ➤ How do you handle unexpected problems? Are you better at the pop quiz or do you need time to discern and respond?
> ➤ Do you draw strength from outside input or are you more comfortable setting the tone by speaking before others?
> ➤ When a crisis lands in your lap, is your first instinct avoidance or exploration?

> ➤ Are you more likely to join in the negative reactions of others to setbacks or to take a step back to reflect on what's occurring?

At a personal level, a key element of this competency is your ability to pause when chaos is all around you. When the noise of crisis is rising, you must seek the space to rise above it and view the landscape. Chances are, there is a role model in your world who does this well. If you ask me that question, a few people immediately come to mind. I know they weren't born that way; they developed this skill. Partly through training, mentoring, and simply as a product of their experiences. Get close to these people in your orbit and let them know you're working on your calm steadiness.

In your company, and particularly on your team, develop this skill by actively modeling it. Taking the hardest circumstances in stride, while cutting through the brush to focus on options and outcomes, requires an open and well-articulated intention. Instill a mindset on your team that forward motion and course correction are your priorities, and retribution for missteps is not part of your management philosophy. Then put it into practice. The collective acceptance and application of these principles will advance this skill on your team, and become part of your leadership identity.

Learning orientation

Key questions:

> ➤ How much do you think you know? Do you sometimes think you have it all figured out? Do you feel naked about the things you don't know? Or are you somewhere in between?

> ➤ Are you a curious person? How often do you ask, *What's up with that?*
> ➤ When you have a formal training opportunity, do you dig in and really participate, or just mail it in?
> ➤ Are you energized by advancing the learning of those around you?

Let's start with you. Twelve years of education followed by four years at business school, perhaps an MBA after that. On average you've completed a formal training course every eighteen months during your career. You've read books, watched and listened to experts, and attended seminars. You've retained some of what you have learned. You can call that learning, but I want more from you. I want you to spend every day as a curious person. Ask why and why not. Every interaction and every dose of new information. Seek answers. But more importantly, seek the next question, then chase the answers. Be opportunistic when a learning opportunity is in front of you, and bring others along. Make learning your mindset, not just ink on your resume.

As a leader in your organization, you have a responsibility. You must uncover the hot spots where your team or your company has a deficit. It might be around time management, customer relationships, or product or industry knowledge. As I said earlier, if you have a gap in these and other areas critical to your business, chances are that others have the same gap. Be the advocate in your organization that drives formalized training in the subjects where there could be a group learning benefit. Then take the ride with your people and learn more yourself.

Pragmatic resilience

Key questions:

> ➢ Do you hedge your bets or go all in?
> ➢ Do you assess outcomes and then handicap your odds of success? Does that handicapping affect your strategy, or limit your effort?
> ➢ How long does it take you to bounce back from defeat?
> ➢ Do you learn from mistakes, or are you stalled out by them?
> ➢ When others fail, do you pick them up and pull them forward to face the next challenge?
> ➢ Do you put pressure on others to go undefeated, or do you accept that setbacks are part of long-term success?

As you rise in your organization, the road gets increasingly lonely. Pragmatic resilience is imperative for survival. The long journey upward will become a short one downward for the leader who cannot master this skill. Seek out your company's available leadership training or executive coaching resources, and gain a senior leader sponsor to guide you along. It's important to broadcast to your executive leadership team that you understand the need for this skill. It may be the one strength that separates the middle manager from the high-potential future executive. If your company doesn't offer adequate internal development, source it outside from a well-established executive leadership training provider.

For yourself, the starting point should center around managing pace. You live in a streaming, on-demand world that allows little opportunity for reflective thought. That revolving life keeps you from discerning, from observing. It keeps you from contextualizing the ups and downs of your leading role. Build time into your schedule for deeper thinking. Make appointments with yourself that distractions and impromptu meetings cannot pierce. Read long-form materials on subjects that relate to your aspirations. Listen to podcasts. Go see a speaker. Step off your ride on a regular basis and rebuild your ability to understand situations holistically. Make choices and take risks from that bigger perspective. Your problems will feel smaller, and your setbacks will too.

Humility

Key questions:

> - Do you think more about taking credit or making credit? About avoiding blame or owning outcomes?
> - Do you walk with a quiet confidence or a campaign sign?
> - Can you allow others the space to view your performance from a distance?
> - Are you managing your own personal public relations machine?
> - Do you worry about what people are thinking about you or do you think about how you can help them?

Let's be honest. Humility is an admirable trait, but if it isn't accompanied by accomplishments, it rarely gets discussed. Nobody ever said, "That guy who fails all the time is so humble." Of course he is. You need to perform before humility really matters. In your company, that performance cannot go unnoticed. From a purely practical standpoint, you need to keep succeeding at your work and someone needs to see you. Find a champion in your organization. Perhaps a member of your senior leadership team. Make a deal with them. You won't go around bragging, if they promise to pay attention to your good works and share their observations with others. Remember, I said you have to have low ego, but not no ego.

In your personal interactions, particularly with your team members, practice learning the details of their work. Become well versed in their successes and challenges. Understand them as whole persons. When you have an opportunity, play the same role for them that you are asking your champion to play for you. Transform your personal public relations machine into one that serves your people. One more thing. Get a good mirror, and look at it once in a while. If you see any self-deception, wipe it clean.

Undoubtedly, as you have read these pages, you have begun identifying the gaps in your own repertoire. You've concluded that while there is room for growth across all these competencies, you need to be practical by choosing a few areas to focus on first. After all, the person who tries to improve everything at once often ends up improving little. So make your selections and get moving!

MY WISH FOR YOU

I am not the person I was yesterday. I am also not the person I was when I began my sales career thirty years ago. Neither are you the person you have been. You are a new person today.

When I think about how much I didn't know on my first day of selling as compared to how much I understand now, it stops me. I'll skip the metaphor. It is immeasurable.

My experiences have resulted in wisdom I could have never predicted. They have also produced curiosities that dwarf that wisdom. I still want to grow and learn. I know that will never stop for me.

If you take one benefit from this book, I hope it is to develop a fearless curiosity to seek understanding. Become the person who embraces not knowing. The person who doesn't marvel over the list of information they possess, but delights in the things they might still learn. The person who engages others with good cheer about picking up new skills, and encourages those around you to do the same. The person who brings new questions to bear when the group declares, "We've got this."

I think I may know you. Not by name, but I know you. You are reading this book because wherever you may be on your trajectory toward compassionate leadership, you are probably standing at a station that I passed through. Perhaps I stopped there. Maybe struggled there. It might be a station where I enjoyed success or endured failure. Or one I wish I could revisit. One where I learned a life-giving lesson. I know you. And now you know me.

I believe in you. You picked up this book because you are striving. You strive because you matter in the lives of other people. You believe there is a noble way to lead others. A compassionate way. I believe in this purpose that you and I share.

It is my wish for you that you develop relationships with people who care deeply about you and your development as a compassionate leader. As the leader who will bring your own approach to leading effectively while improving the lives of those around you.

Make no mistake. Business is about winning. But it is not about defeating others in that endeavor. There is abundance. Enough for everybody. Your role as The Modern Compassionate Leader is to create as many winners as you can. Do that by working on improving yourself across these twelve dimensions and bring others along with you.

I've seen it in action. I've lived it. So can you.

Lead well, my friend.

Acknowledgments

So many deserve thanks in helping me to produce this, my first book.

My wife Kathy and children Kayleigh, Megan, and Will are my unconditional cheerleaders. They have been along for the ride from the genesis of a thin idea to the finished product. Love you.

My siblings have long been my backstop for clear thinking and looking at life through a lens colored with good humor. Thank you Denny, Sally, Nancy, Kevin, and Bridget.

My parents Bill and Kay Martin gave me a childhood that continues to pay me rewards in the form of fond memories. Dad passed way too early and Mom has been the model of how to carry on with dignity. Nobody is luckier than I.

My extended family brings me joy and support beyond what I deserve. So many good souls, I think of you often.

I'm grateful for the hundreds of good people I've worked with through my career. Too many to name, I've had the great fortune of forming fulfilling relationships throughout my work life. I hold you each in my heart.

My friends and other supporters have been so gracious to allow me the space to share my dream and listen to my ideas. I am grateful to you.

My great thanks to my editor Alexandra O'Connell, who helped me turn my raw thoughts into a professional work. Also, thanks to my friends at Lighthouse Writers Workshop, my instructor Joel Warner, and my fellow aspiring writers. You helped me believe that writing could become my primary vocation.

Finally, thank you, the aspiring compassionate leader. You are my inspiration and the reason I wrote this book. I hope it serves for you as the resource I wished I had when I was in your shoes.

Suggested Reading

Allen, David. *Getting Things Done: The Art of Stress-Free Productivity*. New York: Penguin Putnam, 2001.

Arbinger Institute, The. *Leadership and Self-Deception: Getting Out of the Box*. San Francisco: Berrett-Koehler Publishers, 2002.

Badaracco Jr., Joseph L. *Leading Quietly: An Unorthodox Guide to Doing the Right Thing*. Boston: Harvard Business School Press, 2002.

Bakke, Dennis. *The Decision Maker: Unlock the Potential of Everyone in Your Organization, One Decision at a Time*. Seattle, WA: Pear Press, 2013.

Bangley, Bernard. *Authentic Devotion: Introduction to the Devout Life by Francis de Sales*. Colorado Springs, CO: WaterBrook Press, 2002.

Blanchard, Kenneth and Spencer Johnson. *The One Minute Manager*. New York: HarperCollins, 2000.

Bossidy, Larry and Ram Charan. *Execution: The Discipline of Getting Things Done*. New York: Crown Business, 2002.

Bradberry, Travis and Jean Greaves. *Emotional Intelligence 2.0*. San Diego, CA: TalentSmart, 2009.

Brooks, David. *The Road to Character*. New York: Random House, 2015.

Brown, Brene. *Daring Greatly: How the Courage to Be Vulnerable Transforms the Way We Live, Love, Parent, and Lead*. New York: Penguin Group, 2012.

Carew, Jack. *The Mentor: 15 Keys to Success in Sales, Business, and Life*. New York: Penguin Putnam, 1998.

Case, John. *Open-Book Management: The Coming Business Revolution*. New York: HarperCollins, 1996.

Christensen, Clayton M. and Michael E. Raynor. *The Innovator's Solution: Creating and Sustaining Successful Growth*. Boston: Harvard Business Review Press, 2003.

Collins, Jim. *How the Mighty Fall: And Why Some Companies Never Give In*. New York: HarperCollins, 2009.

Cooperrider, David L. *Appreciative Inquiry: A Positive Revolution in Change*. Oakland, CA: Berrett-Koehler Publishers, 2005. Kindle edition.

Corbett, David. *Portfolio Life: The New Path to Work, Purpose, and Passion After 50*. San Francisco, CA: Jossey-Bass, 2007.

Department of the Army. "A Leader's Guide to After-Action Reviews." Washington, DC: U.S. Army Combined Arms Command, 2003. Accessed April 4, 2017. http://www.au.af.mil/au/awc/awcgate/army/tc_25-20/tc25-20.pdf.

Doran, George T. "There's a S.M.A.R.T. Way to Write Management's Goals and Objectives." *Management Review* 70, no. 11 (1981): 35-36. Accessed April 4, 2017. http://community.mis.temple.edu/mis0855002fall2015/files/2015/10/S.M.A.R.T-Way-Management-Review.pdf.

Eisner, Michael D. and Aaron R. Cohen. *Working Together: Why Great Partnerships Succeed.* New York: HarperCollins, 2010.

Ferrazzi, Keith and Tahl Raz. *Never Eat Alone: and other Secrets to Success, One Relationship at a Time.* New York: Doubleday, 2005.

Flaum, Sander A. and Jonathon A. Flaum. *The 100-Mile Walk: A Father and Son on a Quest to Find the Essence of Leadership.* New York: AMACON Books, 2006.

Freedman, David H. *Corps Business: The 30 Management Principles of the U.S. Marines.* New York: HarperCollins, 2000.

Harvey, Jerry B. *The Abilene Paradox: And Other Meditations on Management.* San Francisco: Jossey-Bass, 1988.

Kahneman, Daniel. *Thinking, Fast and Slow.* New York: Farrar, Straus and Giroux, 2013.

Keim, Brandon. "Thinking in a Foreign Language Makes Decisions More Rational." WIRED. Published April 24, 2012, https://www.wired.com/2012/04/language-and-bias/.

Khalsa, Mahan. *Let's Get Real or Let's Not Play: The Demise of Dysfunctional Selling and the Advent of Helping Clients Succeed.* Salt Lake City, UT: White Water Press, 1999.

Kim, W. Chan and Renee Mauborgne. *Blue Ocean Strategy: How to Create Uncontested Market Space and Make the Competition Irrelevant.* Boston: Harvard Business Review Press, 2005.

Kotter, John P. *The Heart of Change: Real-Life Stories of How People Change Their Organizations.* Boston: Harvard Business Review Press, 2012.

Kranz, Gene. *Failure is Not an Option: Mission Control from Mercury to Apollo 13 and Beyond.* New York: Simon & Schuster, 2009.

Lambert, Richard A. *Financial Literacy for Managers: Finance and Accounting for Better Decision-Making.* Philadelphia: Wharton Digital Press, 2012.

Lee, Gus. *Courage: The Backbone of Leadership.* San Francisco: Jossey-Bass, 2006.

Lombardo, Michael M. and Robert W. Eichinger. *For Your Improvement: A Guide for Development and Coaching.* Lominger International, 2009.

Madson, Patricia Ryan. *Improv Wisdom: Don't Prepare, Just Show Up.* New York: Bell Tower, 2010.

Marquardt, Michael. *Leading with Questions: How Leaders Find the Right Solutions by Knowing What to Ask.* San Francisco: Jossey-Bass, 2005.

Maxwell, John C. *Ethics 101: What Every Leader Needs to Know.* New York: Center Street, 2005.

— — —. *The 360° Leader: Developing Your Influence from Anywhere in the Organization.* Nashville, TN: Thomas Nelson, Inc., 2005.

Miller, Robert B. and Stephen E. Heiman. *The New Successful Large Account Management.* New York: Hachette Book Group, 2005.

Morrel, Margot and Capparell, Stephanie. *Shackleton's Way: Leadership Lessons from the Great Antarctic Explorer.* New York: Penguin Putnam, 2001.

Myers, Isabel Briggs and Peter B. Myers. *Gifts Differing: Understanding Personality Type.* Mountain View, CA: CPP, Inc., 1995.

Pink, Daniel H. *Drive: The Surprising Truth About What Motivates Us.* New York: Penguin Group, 2009.

———. "The Puzzle of Motivation." TED.com. Published July 2009, accessed April 2017. https://www.ted.com/talks/dan_pink_on_motivation?language=en.

Rath, Tom. *StrengthsFinder 2.0*. New York: Gallup Press, 2007.

Reynolds, Garr. *Presentation Zen: Simple Ideas on Presentation Design and Delivery*. Berkeley, CA: New Riders, 2008.

Sanborn, Mark. *The Fred Factor: How Passion in your Work and Life Can Turn the Ordinary into the Extraordinary*. New York: Doubleday, 2004.

Sinek, Simon. *Leaders Eat Last: Why Some Teams Pull Together and Others Don't*. New York: Penguin Group, 2014.

Stack, Jack. *The Great Game of Business: The Only Sensible Way to Run a Company*. New York: Crown Business, 2013.

Stanier, Michael Bungay. *The Coaching Habit: Say Less, Ask More & Change the Way You Lead Forever*. Toronto, ON Canada: Box of Crayons Press, 2016.

Watkins, Michael. *The First 90 Days: Critical Success Strategies for New Leaders at All Levels*. Boston: Harvard Business School Press, 2003.

Weissman, Jerry. *Presenting to Win: The Art of Telling Your Story*. Upper Saddle River, NJ: Times Prentice Hall Books, 2003.

Wooden, John. *The Essential Wooden: A Lifetime of Lessons and Leadership*. New York: McGraw-Hill, 2007.

Wilson, Jerry S. and Blumenthal, Ira. *Managing Brand YOU: Seven Steps to Creating Your Most Successful Self*. New York: AMACOM, 2008.

About the Author

Throughout his career, Jim has demonstrated an ability to form and develop high performing sales teams, turn around declining business units, and build newly-formed emerging business segments into growing and profitable businesses. Jim's compassionate leadership style, business acumen, and ability to establish positive relationships with others are the keys to his success. Aligning teams behind clear strategy to produce measurable success is Jim's core passion.

Jim writes and speaks about his experience and insights on the topics of leadership, career development, productivity, selling, and personal empowerment. Jim is particularly interested in the growth of mid-level leaders who are inspiring others while they develop their own leadership strengths.

Jim lives with his family in Broomfield, CO, where they enjoy a variety of outdoor activities and experiences.

You can connect with Jim at JMMLeadership@gmail.com or on Twitter at @JMMLeadership.

To learn more about Jim's approach to leadership
or to hire Jim to speak at your event, visit:
www.ModernCompassionateLeader.com

Endnotes

Chapter Two

1 Keim, "Thinking in a Foreign Language Makes Decisions More Rational."

Chapter Three

2 Freedman, *Corps Business: The 30 Management Principles of the U.S. Marines*, 8-10.

3 Wooden, *The Essential Wooden: A Lifetime of Lessons and Leadership*, 97.

Chapter Four

4 Department of the Army. "A Leader's Guide to After-Action Reviews," 16-21.

Chapter Five

5 Harvey, *The Abilene Paradox and Other Meditations on Management*, 12-14.

6 Pink, "The Puzzle of Motivation." TED.com.

7 Doran, "There's a S.M.A.R.T. Way to Write Management's Goals and Objectives."

Chapter Six

8   Lombardo and Eichinger, *For Your Improvement: A Guide for Development and Coaching*, 211-216.

Chapter Ten

9   Cooperrider, *Appreciative Inquiry: A Positive Revolution in Change*, 4-14.

Chapter Eleven

10   *Apollo 13*, directed by Ron Howard (1995; Universal City, CA: Universal Home Video, 1998), DVD.

11   Morrell and Capparell, *Shackleton's Way: Leadership Lessons from the Great Atlantic Explorer*, 129-156.

Chapter Twelve

12   *Merriam-Webster Online*, s.v. "humility," accessed April 4, 2017, http://www.merriam-webster.com/dictionary/humility.

13   *Miracle*, directed by Gavin O'Connor (2004; Burbank, CA: Walt Disney Studios Home Entertainment, 2011), Blu-ray.